Kindle® Paperwhite

FOR DUMMIES®

A Wiley Brand

2nd Edition

by Leslie H. Nicoll

Kindle® Paperwhite For Dummies,® 2nd Edition

Published by:
John Wiley & Sons, Inc.
111 River Street
Hoboken, NJ 07030-5774
www.wiley.com

Contents at a Glance

Table of Contents

Introduction

For many, the Kindle family of e-readers has "rekindled" their love of reading. Whether it's the convenience of having an entire library stored on a 7.3-ounce device or the capability to enlarge the font so you can read more comfortably, Kindle users seem to be unanimous in their praise for this handy gadget. Even people uncertain about the idea of an e-reader tend to get hooked after they lay their eyes on the crisp, clear e-ink display — one that truly mimics a printed reading experience.

If you're new to the Kindle world, welcome to the club. If you're a seasoned pro who's owned every generation of the device, I'm pleased to count you among the readership. And if you fall somewhere in between, well, I'm glad you're here, too. My motto is, "Kindle enthusiasts, unite!" I'm here because of my love of reading, and I've discovered that Kindle e-readers, particularly the Kindle Paperwhite, make reading *better*. How? That's what I share with you in this book.

About This Book

The Kindle Paperwhite is so easy to use, you might wonder why you need a book describing how to use it. Good question! Let's just say that in five years of Kindle ownership — and buying every new e-ink Kindle the minute it hits the market — I still discover some new quirk or trick with every device. I share those hard-to-discover secrets in the book, saving you time and effort. In addition, reviewing the basics is always helpful, so I cover those in the book as well.

The chapters are designed so that they can stand alone — if you don't feel like you need a primer on tapping and swiping, skip ahead to something that interests you more. Looking for free books? See Chapter 5. Have you heard that you can rent textbooks? That process is explained in Chapter 9. Is your battery not lasting as long as you expect? Discover troubleshooting hints in Chapter 11.

I used certain conventions to make it easy for readers to understand the techniques that are presented, whether they're shortcuts or keywords for searching the Kindle Store:

- **Bold:** Indicates an action you take on the touchscreen. The bold, numbered text in a numbered list indicates the action you take to accomplish a task. Similarly, if you need to type something using the on screen keyboard, those instructions will be printed in bold.

- *Italics:* Indicates a term I define. I also use italics to indicate a term you search for on the web. Italics are also used to indicate placeholder text, such as *yourname*@free.kindle.com and *yourname*@kindle.com.

- `Monofont`: Indicates a *URL* (a web address). Note that URLs are links; just tap the URL with your finger to go to that web page — if you're reading this on your Kindle Paperwhite, of course!

In addition to URLs, chapter and section references are links; just tap the chapter title or section listing to select it and the device instantly jumps to the place you chose.

Foolish Assumptions

This book was written about the newest e-ink Kindle, known as the Kindle Paperwhite (second generation), which was released on September 30, 2013. I assume that's the Kindle version you own, or at least have access to, to try out the tips, tricks, and procedures that I discuss.

I assume that you have some sort of computer (Windows or Mac) that has a USB port so that you can connect your Kindle Paperwhite to the port with the USB cable that ships with the device.

I don't expect you to be a computer genius. However, I assume that you know how to navigate on your computer, search the web, tell the difference between files and folders, and copy and paste items from one place to another.

I assume that you're familiar with Amazon and have an active account there to which you can log in and purchase content.

Icons Used in This Book

For Dummies titles use icons to highlight information. Look for the following icons in this book:

Quick hints, helpful tips, and other tidbits of information are included in the paragraphs that are highlighted with the bull's-eye and arrow.

Tie a string on your finger and keep these things in mind. Remember items are mostly gleaned from my experience.

Although it's hard to break a Kindle Paperwhite, you can do things inadvertently that you might not be able to undo, such as permanently delete a favorite e-book. These pitfalls are highlighted with the little bomb in the Warning icon.

Occasionally, I provide details of interest to the technically curious. This nitty-gritty information is flagged with the Technical Stuff icon.

Where to Go from Here

This book is clear, practical, down-to-earth, and full of helpful hints. I've written 12 chapters, but you don't need to read them in order — each chapter stands on its own. So if you're interested in a particular topic, jump ahead to that chapter.

Have fun exploring your Kindle Paperwhite. For most activities, it's an intuitive and user-friendly device. This book helps you get started and guides you to some of the more advanced features that the Kindle Paperwhite offers. Tap the screen on your Kindle Paperwhite to advance to the next page and keep reading, or use the helpful links in the text and in the table of contents to jump to the section or chapter that covers a particular topic that interests you.

If you want to go deeper with your Kindle Paperwhite experience, consider joining an online Kindle forum. You'll be able to share tips, e-book recommendations, and more with thousands of other Kindle owners.

Your Kindle Paperwhite opens a new world of reading, with vast libraries of e-books at your fingertips. Enjoy the trip!

Chapter 1

Hello, Kindle Paperwhite

In This Chapter

▶ Figuring out which version of the Kindle Paperwhite you want

▶ Taking a short history class

▶ Finding out why your device is a delight

*W*elcome to the wonderful world of Kindle reading. Getting started with your Kindle Paperwhite is quick and easy. This chapter introduces the basic features of the Kindle Paperwhite and discusses the first steps in becoming a successful *Kindler* — a Kindle user and reader.

Choosing a Kindle Paperwhite

Before you purchase your Kindle Paperwhite, you need to consider the following:

✔ **How you connect to the Internet:** Decide whether you want to connect to the Internet using only Wi-Fi (the Kindle Paperwhite) or Wi-Fi plus 3G (the Kindle Paperwhite 3G).

Throughout this book, I use *Kindle Paperwhite* when referring to both models. When I need to differentiate between the two models, I call them the Wi-Fi–only Kindle Paperwhite and the Kindle Paperwhite 3G.

✔ **Whether you want offers and ads on your screensaver:** You can purchase a Kindle Paperwhite that has special offers and sponsored screensavers, or you can buy one with traditional screensavers, which do not display advertising.

Mixing and matching among these choices gives you four versions of the Kindle Paperwhite:

✔ Wi-Fi–only Kindle Paperwhite with special offers and sponsored screensavers ($119)

- Wi-Fi–only Kindle Paperwhite with traditional screensavers — that is, no special offers and no advertising ($139)

- Kindle Paperwhite 3G with special offers and sponsored screensavers ($189)

- Kindle Paperwhite 3G with traditional screensavers ($209)

In this section, I help you choose your best Kindle Paperwhite.

A brief Kindle history

The first Amazon Kindle became available in November 2007 and sold out in less than six hours. Many users back-ordered their Kindles and waited months to receive them. The following year, when Oprah Winfrey announced on her television show that the Kindle was her "new favorite gadget," sales skyrocketed, and again, the Kindle went out of stock. For two years in a row, the Kindle wasn't available for Christmas shopping!

At a press conference in 2009, Jeff Bezos, accompanied by author Stephen King, announced the second-generation Kindle. Also in 2009, the Kindle DX — the larger Kindle — and Kindle applications for the PC, Mac, and iPhone became available. To the joy of readers around the globe, an international version of the Kindle also came out in the fall of that year.

The third-generation Kindle, known as the Kindle Keyboard, became available in 2010; it was the first Kindle offered with Wi-Fi only or Wi-Fi plus 3G. A few months after it was released, Amazon started offering a version of the device with special offers and sponsored screensavers.

The Kindle had a windfall year in 2011, with three new devices announced and released in a two-month span: a basic Wi-Fi –only model, the Kindle Touch, and an Android tablet called the Kindle Fire. One of the most exciting innovations at that time was the introduction of a touchscreen for the e-ink family of readers.

Kindle had another banner year in 2012, with the debut of a number of devices with more options, including the Kindle Paperwhite, which was the first e-ink Kindle with a built-in light.

The second-generation Paperwhite was released in October 2013. The latest device has better contrast, darker text, and page turns that are 25 percent faster than its predecessor.

Wi-Fi only versus Wi-Fi plus 3G

How do you decide whether you want a Wi-Fi–only Kindle Paperwhite or the Kindle Paperwhite 3G? Good question!

The Wi-Fi –only Kindle Paperwhite requires a Wi-Fi wireless connection to download content from Amazon and other sources. If you have Wi-Fi set up in your home, you can use it as your Wi-Fi hotspot. You can connect your Kindle Paperwhite also to Wi-Fi hotspots in public locations, such as Starbucks and McDonald's.

The Kindle Paperwhite 3G operates not only on Wi-Fi but also on the same cellular network as cellphones. In essence, the device is available to you everywhere — in your home, office, and car as well as in public areas such as airports, train stations, and restaurants. Although 3G is widely available, some places in the United States don't have coverage. Amazon provides a coverage map, which can be accessed at `www.amazon.com/gp/help/customer/display.html?nodeId=200375890&#whispintl`.

Best of all, the Kindle Paperwhite 3G, unlike a cellphone, accrues no additional charges for 3G coverage. Amazon covers the 3G costs.

If you anticipate needing to use only wireless — at home or connected to another Wi-Fi network — the Wi-Fi–only Kindle Paperwhite is a good choice. On the other hand, if you don't have access to Wi-Fi, you travel regularly, or you just love the magic of being able to download an e-book in less than a minute, anywhere, any time, you may prefer the Kindle Paperwhite 3G.

Special offers and sponsored screensavers

In 2011, Amazon came out with a new option: special offers and sponsored screensavers — in other words, advertising on Kindle e-readers. In exchange for this, Amazon discounted the price of the device — at present, a $20 discount on the price of the Kindle Paperwhite. On online forums, users' reactions to this change have been mixed, but mostly positive. Those who are opposed don't like having advertising on their Kindle Paperwhite, period. On the other hand, many appreciate the discounts and special offers on Kindle e-books and accessories as well as on other products, such as clothing and electronics sold through Amazon. The special offers appear as screensavers and on a small bar at the bottom of the Home screen. No advertising occurs in content on the Kindle Paperwhite.

If you choose a Kindle Paperwhite with special offers and decide you don't like them, you can unsubscribe for $20 — the difference in the price that you paid originally. Go to the Manage Your Kindle page for your Amazon account (www.amazon.com/myk), choose Manage Your Devices, and tap Edit in the Special Offers column to unsubscribe. You may resubscribe later at no additional cost if you want, but you will not receive a refund.

The $20 charge does not include sales tax (for those states that tax Amazon purchases).

If you choose a device that includes special offers, the screensaver changes regularly. Some people, even if they don't take advantage of the discounts, like the variety of pictures. Traditional Kindle Paperwhite screensavers — that is, with no special offers — display a variety of graphics related to printing, publishing, and writing, such as pen nibs and blocks of type.

For international readers

The Kindle was released in November 2007, but international customers had to wait two long years before they could buy a Kindle in their country. The latest generation Paperwhite, however, is sold in the United Kingdom, Europe, and Japan through the Amazon store specific to each country. For example, the figure shows the Japanese model, with Kanji letters.

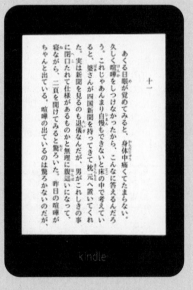

To find out more, visit:

- ✔ United Kingdom: www.amazon.co.uk (released October 9, 2013)
- ✔ Europe: www.amazon.de (released October 9, 2013)
- ✔ Japan: www.amazon.co.jp (released October 22, 2013)

Note that the Kindle Paperwhite sold in these countries is available as Wi-Fi only or Wi-Fi plus 3G, but without special offers and sponsored screensavers.

The Paperwhite Screen

Weighing 7.3 or 7.6 ounces (the 3G model is a tiny bit heavier), with a 6-inch-high display, the Kindle Paperwhite provides 2GB (approximately 1.25 GB available for personal content) of e-book storage (and free Cloud storage for all Amazon content), enough to store approximately 1,100 e-books and other content. With wireless turned off, the light set at 10, and a half-hour of daily reading, the battery charge can last up to two months.

Touchscreen technology

The touchscreen technology introduced in the Kindle Touch has been further developed and refined in the latest generation of the Kindle Paperwhite.

The screen on the device uses capacitive technology, which means that very light touches with your finger — or a capacitive stylus — will cause changes on the screen.

Note that you must use a bare finger or a stylus to use the touchscreen.

The Kindle screen is delicate. Placing heavy objects on top of your Kindle, especially those with sharp edges, can damage the screen. Dropping your Kindle can also break the screen. To protect their investment, many people use covers and screen protectors on their device. (See Chapter 10 for more about covers and other accessories.)

Let your light shine

The Kindle Paperwhite builds on the best of the past and adds a number of innovations. The improvement that is generating the most buzz is its built-in light.

Before the introduction of the first Kindle Paperwhite in 2012, readers had to use an external light source — the sun, a lamp, or a portable reading light. On a Kindle Paperwhite, however, the light is sandwiched between the layers of the screen and shines toward the surface of the e-ink display. As a result, the light does not shine in your eyes as it does with a backlit device, such as a tablet or a smartphone. The result? Less eyestrain for you and an overall even distribution of light on the screen. The screen and light make reading in any lighting condition a pleasure.

You can adjust the light for different lighting conditions by using the Light icon on the toolbar. For details, see Chapter 3.

Figure 1-1 illustrates the components that make up the light, touch-screen, and display. When describing the screen, users note that it seems very white, almost like paper, and the letters look like they're floating on the display. The contrast of the fonts against the display is darker, too, resulting in a superior reading experience.

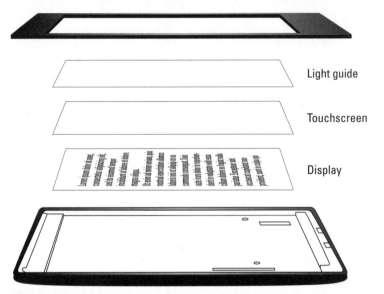

Light guide

Touchscreen

Display

Figure 1-1: The light technology of the Kindle Paperwhite.

The e-ink screen

The Kindle was one of the first widely available commercial e-readers to use e-ink in its screen display. E-ink is fundamentally different from an LCD screen, such as those found on a laptop, smartphone, and computer.

With e-ink, thousands of microcapsules of ink are held between two layers of polymer. Reversing the electronic charge changes the capsules from positive to negative, which changes the color from light to dark and, ultimately, results in the display on the screen.

E-ink requires little power, which is why the Kindle battery can hold a charge for up to two months with 30 minutes of reading per day and the light set at 10. In addition, e-ink isn't backlit, which is less fatiguing for your eyes, and it more closely mimics a paper reading experience—that is, looking at ink on the printed page. Furthermore, unlike an LCD screen, a Kindle Paperwhite can be read in bright sunlight without glare or loss of display.

Chapter 2

First Things First

In This Chapter
- Turning on the device
- Selecting a language for the device
- Connecting to Wi-Fi
- Registering your Kindle Paperwhite
- Changing names
- Putting your device to sleep
- Charging!
- Understanding firmware updates

Are you ready to get started with your Kindle Paperwhite? Of course you are. In this chapter, you turn on the device for the first time, register it, and connect it to Wi-Fi. You also find out how to register your Kindle Paperwhite and give it a fun name, the differences between off and sleep, and some basics about the firmware that runs the device.

Making Your Kindle Paperwhite Come Alive

Your Kindle Paperwhite arrives in a simple black box that belies the magic that lies inside. Pull off the tear strip, open the box — perhaps ooh and aah a bit — and then, let's get started!

Over the next few pages, you will be doing the following:

- Turning on the device
- Selecting a language
- Turning on Wi-Fi
- Registering your Kindle Paperwhite

First things first: Turn on the Kindle Paperwhite by pressing and then releasing the power button.

Figure 2-1 illustrates the bottom of the device, where you'll find the power button as well as the USB port. The power button is the only physical button on the entire device.

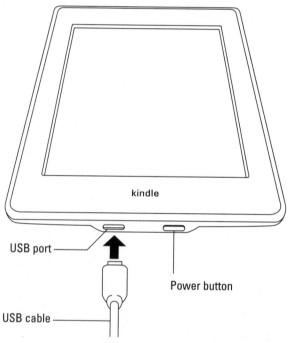

kindle

USB port

Power button

USB cable

Figure 2-1: The bottom edge of the Kindle Paperwhite.

If this is the first time you're using your Kindle Paperwhite, it will initiate a booting process, which will take a few minutes to complete.

The first option that you will see, after the logo is displayed, is a screen for choosing the language for your Kindle Paperwhite. On to the next section!

Selecting a Language

Following along from the preceding section, your next task is to select a language. After powering on your device, it displays the screen shown in Figure 2-2.

Deutsch	Français (Canada)
English (United Kingdom)	Italiano
English (United States)	日本語
Español	Português (Brasil)
Español (México)	简体中文
Français	

Figure 2-2: Select a language here.

Tap the language you want to use for the device, and then tap Next.

If you want English but would prefer to see the time displayed using a 24-hour clock (for example, 3 p.m. will appear as 15:00), choose English (UK).

After you tap Next, the device finishes booting in the language you've chosen and the Kindle Paperwhite introduction screen appears, as shown in Figure 2-3. Tap Get Started to move to the next step.

Note that you can change your language choice at any time by tapping Menu⇨Settings⇨Device Options⇨Language and Dictionaries⇨Language.

Next up, connecting to a Wi-Fi network.

kindle paperwhite

First-ever Paperwhite display

High Contrast

High Resolution

Built-in Light

Eight weeks battery life
even with the light on

Get Started >

Figure 2-3: Hello, Kindle Paperwhite.

Setting Up Wi-Fi

All versions of the Kindle Paperwhite include Wi-Fi; 3G is an additional option. If you have a Wi-Fi–only Kindle Paperwhite, you need to set up Wi-Fi to receive e-books and content wirelessly.

If no Wi-Fi network is in range, you can add a network later by tapping the x in the upper-right corner of the Wi-Fi Networks dialog box and then tapping Complete Kindle Setup Later.

If you do not connect to a Wi-Fi network and you do not have a 3G Kindle Paperwhite (see Chapter 1 for a discussion of the different types of devices), you will not be able to complete the registration process, the step after setting up Wi-Fi. You can register your device manually, as detailed later in this chapter.

If you have a Kindle Paperwhite 3G, you don't have to set up Wi-Fi to receive content — 3G works automatically without any additional setup. Still, if you have a Wi-Fi hotspot in your home or office, you probably want to go ahead and get it working, just for convenience.

Do you want to send documents to your Kindle Paperwhite 3G through e-mail? If you do so using 3G, Amazon will charge you a small fee. (See Chapter 7 for details.) Documents transferred by e-mail using Wi-Fi are free. Another good reason to set up Wi-Fi!

To set up Wi-Fi, you need to know whether the network is password-protected. Home and office networks are usually password-protected. Wi-Fi hotspots in public locations, such as Starbucks and McDonald's, are generally not secured with a password.

To add a Wi-Fi network to your Kindle Paperwhite, follow these steps:

1. **If necessary, turn on your Kindle Paperwhite.**

2. **Tap Menu⇨Settings.**

3. **From the Settings screen, tap Wi-Fi Networks.**

   If the Kindle Paperwhite is in Airplane mode (that is, Wi-Fi is not turned on), you'll see a message asking if you want to turn off Airplane mode.

4. **If you see the message about turning off Airplane mode, tap OK.**

5. **Select the network to which you want to connect, as shown in Figure 2-4.**

   If the network you want to connect to has a lock icon next to its name, you need to enter a password.

6. **If the network requires a password, enter it in the Wi-Fi Networks dialog box using the onscreen keyboard.**

   If you're connecting to a network at work and don't know the password, see the system administrator.

   You can enter numbers and symbols by tapping the keyboard's 123!? key. Tap ABC to go back to the regular keyboard, as shown in Figure 2-5.

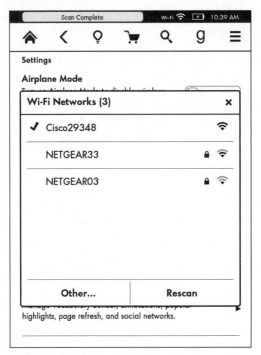

Figure 2-4: My device found this network.

Figure 2-5: This Wi-Fi network requires a password.

Disabling Wi-Fi and 3G

In the Kindle family of devices, you use Airplane mode to disable both Wi-Fi and 3G. (Smartphones use the same method and terminology.)

To turn Airplane mode on and off, tap Menu⇨Settings⇨Airplane Mode. The button to the right is an on/off switch. When Airplane mode is enabled, a plane icon appears next to the battery charge indicator. When it is turned off, you see the wireless indicator (Wi-Fi or 3G).

When you're on a plane, Airplane mode must be enabled for the entire flight. You're allowed to use your Kindle Paperwhite for reading after the plane reaches an altitude of 10,000 feet and the pilot gives the okay. The Paperwhite itself must be turned off for takeoff and landing and anytime the plane is flying at less than 10,000 feet.

If you are unable to connect to Wi-Fi, see Chapter 11 for steps on adding a network manually.

When your Kindle Paperwhite is connected to Wi-Fi, a wireless indicator appears in the upper-right corner of the screen, next to the battery charge meter. You see this indicator on the Home screen and when you display the toolbar while reading an e-book.

The wireless indicator can be one of the following icons:

✔ **Wi-Fi:** The Kindle Paperwhite is connected to a Wi-Fi network. The arcs on the fan next to *Wi-Fi* indicate the strength of the Wi-Fi connection.

✔ **3G:** The Kindle Paperwhite 3G is connected to a 3G network. This icon pertains only to the Kindle Paperwhite that includes 3G and Wi-Fi. The bars next to *3G* indicate the strength of the 3G connection.

✔ **1X:** The Kindle Paperwhite 3G is connected to a network through EDGE/GPRS (the predecessor to 3G in cellular network delivery). The 1X icon applies only to the Kindle Paperwhite 3G. As cellular networks become more widespread, you will rarely — if ever — see this icon.

Your final step is to register your device. Read on.

Registering Your Kindle Paperwhite

If you bought your Kindle Paperwhite through Amazon, it's delivered to you already registered. However, if you bought the Kindle Paperwhite from a store (such as Target, Staples, or Best Buy) or received it as a gift, you need to register it.

If you need to register your device, you'll see the screen shown in Figure 2-6 after you've set up Wi-Fi (see the preceding section).

Figure 2-6: Register your Kindle Paperwhite at Amazon.

If you have an Amazon account, tap the Use an Existing Amazon Account option. Enter your Amazon account e-mail and password. (The Kindle Paperwhite inputs its own serial number, so you don't need to enter it.) Tap Register.

If you don't have an Amazon account:

1. **Tap Create a New Account.**

2. **Choose Country or Region from the menu that appears and then tap Continue.**

3. **Enter your full name, your e-mail address, and a password. Confirm the password and then tap Create Account.**

4. **Enter a payment method and billing address.**

   You need to set up a payment method for your account to purchase from the Kindle Store. The payment method can be a credit card or a gift card purchased from Amazon.

5. **Tap Continue Setup.**

If you have social networks associated with your Amazon account, you'll be asked to verify that you want to connect those to your Kindle. You'll also have an opportunity to set parental controls. You can do both activities later.

That's it! You can now buy books and other content from Amazon and have them delivered wirelessly to your Kindle Paperwhite. If you've purchased content while waiting for your Kindle Paperwhite to arrive, those e-books will appear on the Home screen after the wireless is turned on and the device registers itself.

After the registration process is complete, a short tutorial will begin, showing you the basics of navigating the touchscreen. Don't worry if you forget some of the details they present — the same information and much more is covered in the following pages.

When the tutorial finishes, you see the Home screen, which lists a welcome letter, the Kindle User's Guide, and two built-in dictionaries: the *New Oxford American Dictionary* and the *Oxford Dictionary of English.* (For details on changing dictionaries, see Chapter 8.) Any content you have purchased will also be displayed.

If you ever need to deregister and then re-register your device, the following steps will guide you through the process.

1. **Make sure the wireless is turned on.**

2. **Tap Menu⇨Settings⇨Registration.**

   When you tap Registration, if your Kindle Paperwhite is already registered, you'll see a warning that you are about to deregister your Kindle Paperwhite. Tap Cancel to stop this process.

3. **Choose to register using an existing Amazon account.**

4. **Enter your Amazon login credentials (your account e-mail and password), and tap Register.**

Changing Your Paperwhite's Name

By default, your Kindle Paperwhite is named *Your Name*'s 1st Kindle, where *Your Name* is your first name. This name appears in the upper-left corner of the Home screen. You can change this name, if you want, to something more interesting or fun. For example, some people name their Kindles after famous literary characters or authors. Others choose meaningful words, such as Catalyst — the Paperwhite is a *catalyst* for reading. You can change the name from the device itself or from your computer.

To change your Kindle Paperwhite's name from the device, follow these steps:

1. **Tap Menu⇨Settings⇨Device Options.**

2. **Tap Personalize Your Kindle⇨Device Name.**

3. **Using the onscreen keyboard, enter a new name for your Kindle Paperwhite.**

   Some Kindle Paperwhite owners use their name and phone number as their Kindle Paperwhite's name. That way, if they misplace their Kindle Paperwhite, their contact information is prominently displayed on the Home screen for some kindhearted soul who finds the device and wants to return it to its rightful owner.

4. **Tap the Save button to complete the process.**

To change the device name through your Amazon account on your computer, follow these steps:

1. **Go to www.amazon.com/myk.**

2. **If prompted, enter your e-mail address and password.**

3. **Click the Sign In Using Our Secure Server button.**

4. **Click Manage Your Devices, which appears on the left side of the screen.**

   Your Kindle Paperwhite appears in the list of registered devices.

5. **Click Edit next to the Kindle's name.**

6. **In the dialog box that appears, type a new name and then click the Save button.**

You can also add personal information or a message to the Personal Info section of the Settings menu, as shown in Figure 2-7.

For example, you might add "This Kindle Paperwhite belongs to *your name.* If found, please call *xxx-xxx-xxxx.*"

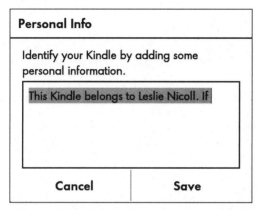

Figure 2-7: Adding a message to identify your Kindle Paperwhite.

To add information or a message, follow these steps:

1. **On the Kindle Paperwhite, tap the Menu icon.**

2. **Tap Settings➪Personalize Your Kindle➪Personal Info.**

3. **Use the onscreen keyboard to enter the desired information.**

4. **Tap Save.**

Note that this information appears only in the Personal Info section — not on the Home screen — and won't be readily apparent to anyone who happens to be looking at your Kindle Paperwhite.

Power Modes: On, Sleep, and Off

The Kindle Paperwhite has three modes for those times when you are not reading it:

✔ **On:** To turn on the Kindle Paperwhite, press and release the power button. On a device without special offers, you see the page that you last viewed before the device went into Sleep mode or was turned off. On a Kindle Paperwhite with special offers, you see the swipe-screen version of the current special offer. Swipe the screen (or tap the bottom of the screen) to go to the page you were on when the device went into Sleep mode or was turned off.

✔ **Sleep:** To put the Kindle Paperwhite in Sleep mode, press and release the power button. A screensaver appears on the display.

✔ **Off:** To turn off the Kindle Paperwhite, press and hold down the power button for five to seven seconds, until the charge indicator light (located next to the power button) blinks. The screen shown in Figure 2-8 appears. Select Screen Off and the screen will go blank.

Until November 2013, passengers were required to turn off their Kindles (all models, including the Kindle Paperwhite) when on a plane during takeoff and landing and anytime the plane was flying at less than 10,000 feet. However, the FAA has recently amended its rules to expand the use of personal electronic devices during all phases of a flight— they hope to provide passengers with a "gate-to-gate" reading, gaming, and video-watching experience. Each airline carrier will be able to decide individually how to implement these new rules on their planes. As a result, things will be "up in the air" for several months as airlines decide how to proceed. The take-away for Kindle-reading passengers is to listen carefully to all announcements from the flight attendants and pilot and, if required, to turn off your Kindle during takeoff and landing.

Power		
Please select from the following options:		
Cancel	Restart	Screen Off

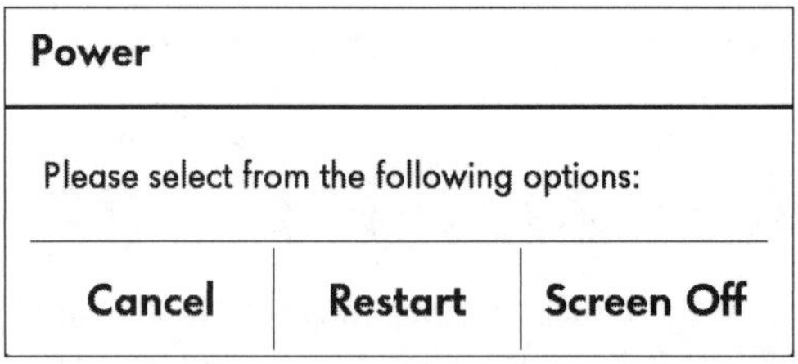

Figure 2-8: Choices when powering off the Paperwhite.

You can easily tell the difference between Sleep and Off modes by the presence (or absence) of a screensaver. A Kindle Paperwhite that is asleep has something displayed on the screen. When turned off, the screen is blank.

The Amazon cover

With the introduction of the Kindle Paperwhite, Amazon announced a new cover with a special feature: Close the cover to put the device in Sleep mode; open the cover to wake up the device. The cover is made of leather and holds the Paperwhite securely in a molded frame.

If you have a Kindle Paperwhite with special offers, when you open the cover it will take you to a special offers screen. Simply swipe the page and your Home screen (or the page you last viewed) appears. (Don't know how to swipe? See Chapter 3.) For other Paperwhites, open the cover and the device displays the Home screen or the page you last viewed.

After ten minutes or so of nonuse, the device goes to sleep and displays a screen-saver. You can wake up the device by pressing the power button or closing and then opening the Amazon cover.

The Kindle Paperwhite uses its battery power only for page turns, so there's no difference in battery usage between putting the device in Sleep mode and turning it off. In general, it's best to simply put the device in Sleep mode instead of turning it off. (The device goes into Sleep mode automatically after ten minutes of inactivity.)

If you want to turn off your Kindle Paperwhite while reading a book, do so from the Home screen. Otherwise, the device may lose your place. This problem doesn't occur when you use Sleep mode, which is another reason why this mode is preferred over completely turning off your Kindle Paperwhite.

Charging Your Device

On the bottom of the Kindle Paperwhite is a micro-USB port for the charging cable (refer to Figure 2-1). The cable has a micro-USB plug on one end and a standard USB plug on the other. Insert the micro-USB plug into the Kindle and the standard USB plug into your computer or into a plug adapter, which is then plugged into an electrical wall socket.

The Kindle Paperwhite doesn't ship with a plug adapter. If you want to use a plug adapter, you must purchase one or use a compatible plug adapter, such as the one that comes with the Kindle 2, Kindle KBoard, or iPhone. In addition, the charger that comes with the Kindle Fire also works with the Kindle Paperwhite. See Chapter 10 for a picture of a plug adapter sold by Amazon.

When the Kindle Paperwhite is plugged into a power source and charging, the charge indicator light (located next to the power button) glows amber. When the device is fully charged, the light turns green.

The first time you charge your Kindle Paperwhite, the process will take about four hours. After that, charging through the USB cable and a computer takes about three hours and charging through the plug adapter takes one to two hours.

 The battery charge meter is in the upper-right corner of the Home screen. I recommend recharging the battery when it has about a quarter of a charge remaining. You don't need to top off the battery on a daily or weekly basis.

You can read and use your Kindle Paperwhite while it charges. When the Kindle Paperwhite is plugged into an electrical socket, the display doesn't change and you can keep reading. However, when the device is plugged into the USB port on a computer, you see the following message:

> If you want to read or shop on your Kindle while continuing to charge over USB, please keep the USB cable attached, but eject your Kindle from your computer.

If you want to read on your Kindle Paperwhite while it's connected to your computer, leave it physically connected (or plugged in) to the USB port but "eject" the device through the operating system. To "eject" your Kindle Paperwhite:

- **In Windows 8:** Connect the Kindle Paperwhite to your computer, right-click the Paperwhite drive icon, and choose Eject from the menu that appears. A notification that it is safe to remove the Paperwhite from the computer appears on your computer screen; ignore this message. Your Kindle Paperwhite will blink and display the last screen viewed.

- **In Windows 7, Vista, and XP:** Either left- or right-click the Safely Remove Hardware icon in the lower-right corner of the taskbar and choose Eject Amazon Kindle. The screen blinks and returns to whatever was open previously.

- **In Mac OS X:** Press ⌘-E. You can also drag the Kindle icon from the desktop to the trash can, or choose File⇨Eject.

Updating Firmware

At the core of your Kindle Paperwhite is a small computer, complete with hardware, software, and a built-in network platform. The software that runs the Kindle Paperwhite is its firmware. *Firmware* is the core that controls how the device works.

Amazon periodically updates the firmware for the device. Generally, firmware updates fix minor bugs and glitches that may not be apparent to the casual user. However, occasionally a major upgrade or new feature is added. For example, with firmware update 2.5, Amazon added the capability to sort e-books into collections, a feature that had been repeatedly requested by users.

To find out which version of the firmware your Kindle is running, follow these steps:

1. **Tap the Menu icon.**

2. **Tap Settings⇨Menu⇨Device Info.**

   The firmware version is listed, along with the serial number and the space available (in megabytes). The newest Kindle Paperwhite is included in the fifth generation of the devices that have been produced, so the firmware version begins with 5. At the time of this writing, the firmware is version 5.4.0.

If an update is available, your Kindle Paperwhite will download it when you turn on the wireless and connect to a network. If you notice a screen that says *Your Kindle Is Updating,* this is what's happening.

If you're curious as to whether a more current update is available, you can check at Amazon:

1. **Go to your Amazon account at www.amazon.com/myk** and log in.

2. **In the left column, choose Manage Your Devices.**

   If a software update is available for your Kindle Paperwhite, a blue *i* in a white circle will be displayed.

3. **If you see the *i* in a circle, click the picture of the Kindle and follow the onscreen instructions to learn more.**

   If updates are available, you'll see instructions for determining whether you need to upgrade the firmware and, if so, how to download and manually update your Kindle Paperwhite, if you want.

You don't have to manually update your Kindle Paperwhite. Necessary updates happen automatically through the wireless connection. Just be aware that if the screen looks different or if you find new features, the device probably went through an automatic update.

Chapter 3

Getting to Know Your Kindle Paperwhite

In This Chapter

▶ Tapping, swiping, and pinching

▶ Becoming familiar with the icons

▶ Touring the Home screen

▶ Using Page Flip to navigate

Your Kindle Paperwhite has exactly one switch: the power switch on its lower edge. There are no buttons for turning pages or accessing menus, as found on earlier generations of Kindles. All navigation is done through the touchscreen, with finger gestures.

In this chapter, you begin by examining the different finger motions as well as where on the screen you use them. With just a few simple motions, you'll be able to open books and other content and quickly navigate from place to place on your Kindle Paperwhite.

Interacting with the Touchscreen

In this section, you discover some techniques for navigation. If you're a seasoned Kindle Touch or previous generation Kindle Paperwhite owner, the following information should be familiar. However, if you're upgrading from a Kindle with buttons or are new to Kindle overall, the following primer will get you started.

Tapping, swiping, and pinching

All common uses of the Kindle Paperwhite — opening books, turning pages, placing bookmarks, and so on — involve a few simple touchscreen gestures, such as finger taps and swipes. For the most part, these gestures are consistent throughout your interaction with the Kindle Paperwhite. (I point out the few cases where the behavior is a bit different than you might expect.)

Unlike Amazon's first generation touchscreen device, the Kindle Paperwhite has a capacitive touchscreen, which means that it responds only to an ungloved finger or a capacitive stylus that mimics a finger's touch. See Chapter 10 for more information on styli.

Tapping

A simple *tap* is the most common gesture you use with the Kindle Paperwhite. See an onscreen button and want to activate it? Tap the button. Viewing the list of books on your device? Tap one to open it.

When you're reading a book or other content, you tap to *page forward* (display the next page), *page backward* (display the previous page), or display a menu of commands. What happens when you tap a book's page depends on which part of the screen you tap; I discuss the three *tap zones* of a displayed page later in this section.

Swiping

Swiping — or sliding — your finger from right to left horizontally or diagonally on the screen causes it to page forward. The motion is akin to flipping a paper page in a printed book. To page backward, reverse the motion with a left-to-right swipe.

When reading a book or other content, you advance the page by swiping or tapping.

If you want to page forward or backward when viewing a list of books on the Home screen, you must swipe, not tap. A tap on the title of a book (or other content) on the Home screen opens the item for reading.

What happened to the Home button?

Every Kindle before the Paperwhite has a physical Home button that returns the device to the Home screen with just a press. On the Kindle Paperwhite, the Home button is now a Home icon (it looks like a house), which appears on a toolbar at the top of the screen.

If you're reading a book or other content and don't see the toolbar, simply tap the top of the screen to make the toolbar appear.

When swiping, you need to move your finger only a short distance. You can probably swipe (or tap) without moving your hands from their reading position.

Long-tapping

For a *long-tap,* also called a *tap and hold,* you touch and hold down on the screen for a few seconds before releasing. In general, a long-tap results in a special action, depending on what you're viewing at the time.

For example, when viewing a book page, you can long-tap on a word to display its definition. When viewing a list of books on the Home screen, a long-tap on a particular book displays such options as adding the book to a collection and reading its description. If you tap and hold down on the title of an e-book sample listed on the Home screen, you can buy the book, read the description, or delete the sample from the device. (Sampling content is discussed in more detail in Chapter 5.)

Pinching and unpinching

When reading a book or other content, place two fingers (or a finger and a thumb) on the touchscreen and slide them closer together. This *pinch* motion decreases the font size. Move your fingers apart — called an *unpinch* — to increase the font size. You need to move your fingers only a small distance to change the font size.

You might see a lag between the pinching and unpinching motions and a change in the text size. Moving your fingers slowly helps.

Touchscreen zones

The Kindle Paperwhite screen is set up with *tap zones,* which are designed to let you turn pages effortlessly with one finger. To get an idea of the location of these zones, see Figure 3-1 (Portrait mode) and Figure 3-2 (Landscape mode).

The three zones shown in the figures work as follows:

- ✔ **Top zone:** This area covers the full width of the screen and is approximately 1.25" high. While reading a book, a tap in the top zone displays a black bar and two toolbars. The title of the book, the Wi-Fi or 3G icon, the battery status, and the time are displayed in the black bar. The top toolbar contains the Home, Back, Light, Store, Search, and Menu icons. The second toolbar contains the Font icon, Go To, X-Ray, Share, and the Bookmark icon. At the bottom of the screen, you see the title of the current section or chapter of the book along with your progress, which can be displayed in locations or pages, as well as the time left in the chapter or book. Just tap in the lower-left corner to cycle through these options. For details, see the next section, "Navigating with Icons."

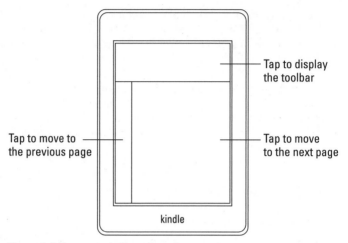

Figure 3-1: Tap zones in Portrait mode.

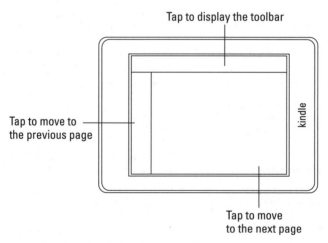

Figure 3-2: Tap zones in Landscape mode.

The top toolbar is always displayed on the Home screen.

✔ **Central zone:** This area, which is the largest of the three zones, covers the middle of the screen to the right of the left zone and below the top zone. A quick tap or swipe here advances to the next page.

✔ **Left zone**: This area is a long, narrow rectangle approximately .5" wide. A tap in the left column moves to the previous page. Because this zone is narrow, your tapping has to be precise. That said, if you can visualize the zone on the screen, remembering where to tap will be easier.

To put your Kindle Paperwhite in Landscape mode, tap Menu➪ Landscape Mode. Note that Landscape mode is accessible only while in a book.

Navigating with Icons

The Kindle Paperwhite has one physical button on the device: the power button. Buttons that were on earlier versions of the Kindle, such as Home, Back, and Font, are incorporated as icons in toolbars on the screen. These virtual buttons are described in this section.

Toolbars when viewing a book

When you open a book and advance through its pages, you see the text on the page and progress information at the bottom of the screen. That's it! But if you tap in the top zone on the screen, you see the toolbars shown in Figure 3-3. The icons displayed on these toolbars are described in the next section.

Home icon

The Home icon always brings you back to the Home screen, no matter where you are or what you've tapped. Consider this icon your virtual friend.

Back icon

The Back icon, like the Back icon in a web browser, lets you retrace your steps. In some instances, the Back icon acts like the Home icon. For example, if you open a book from the Home screen, read a few pages, and then tap the Back icon, you return to the Home screen — not the previous page you looked at.

In a newspaper or magazine, however, the Back icon works differently. See the "Toolbars when viewing periodicals" section for details.

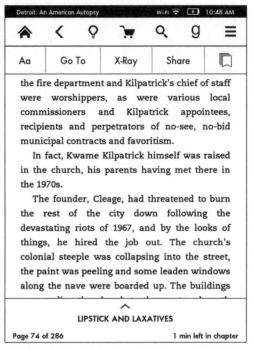

Figure 3-3: The toolbars you see when reading a book.

Light icon

The Light icon controls the built-in light. Tap this icon to display the adjustment meter shown in Figure 3-4. The light gradient has 24 levels, from very dim (1) to very bright (24). To adjust the light, tap the plus or minus sign on either end of the meter or tap on the meter itself. Play with the adjustment meter in different lighting conditions to see what works best for you.

Note that the screen says, "In brightly lit rooms, use a high setting," and "Use a low setting for dark rooms." This advice might seem counterintuitive, but it is correct. When your eyes become accustomed to a dark room, your pupils are dilated and you need less light to see. Too bright a light can be painful. In bright light, your pupils are constricted and thus need more light to see.

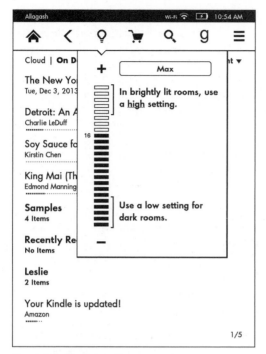

Figure 3-4: The light adjustment meter.

Store icon

Tapping the Store icon takes you to the Amazon Kindle Store. If wireless is turned off, you'll be prompted to activate it. Note that the icon appears dimmed if you've turned off access to the Kindle Store under Parental Controls.

Parental controls allow you to disable access to the web browser, the Kindle Store, and the Cloud. In addition, when parental controls are enabled, you cannot deregister or reset your Kindle Paperwhite. You might want to disable these features to prevent others who might be using your Kindle Paperwhite, such as your children, from making unauthorized purchases. You might also want to prevent others from seeing what you have purchased by viewing your content in the Cloud. To access this feature, tap Menu⇨Settings⇨Device Options⇨Parental Controls. Parental controls — and other kid-conscious features — are discussed in detail in Chapter 9.

If you have a Wi-Fi–only Kindle Paperwhite and are not in an area with a Wi-Fi hotspot, you can't connect to the Kindle Store.

Search icon

When you tap the Search icon, the screen displays a Search page. Use the onscreen keyboard to type a search term in the search field.

To the left of the search field is a drop-down menu. (By default, the menu says My Items if you're on the Home page.) Tap the arrow to display your menu choices: My Items, All Text, Kindle Store, Dictionary, and Wikipedia. Within a book or a periodical, you can also restrict your search to just the book or periodical by selecting This Book or This Issue. To search the Kindle Store or Wikipedia, the device must be connected to Wi-Fi.

When you change the search parameter (for example, selecting All Text from the drop-down menu), that choice remains in force until you change it again.

Goodreads icon

When you tap the Goodreads icon, the screen displays the built-in Goodreads app. You can look at updates from your friends, view your own shelves, or see what your friends are reading. You can also add books from your Amazon account, and mark them as read, currently reading, or want to read. For books that you've finished, you can rate them from one to five stars.

The Goodreads app is discussed in more detail under social networks in Chapter 8.

If you don't have a Goodreads account, you'll be prompted to create one using your Amazon login credentials.

Menu icon

The Menu icon is probably what you tap most often when using your Kindle Paperwhite. I discuss specific uses of the Menu icon throughout this book — turning on and off the wireless, finding the settings on your device, or reading annotations and notes. If you're wondering how to do something, no matter what it might be, tap the Menu icon first. To close a menu, tap the X in the upper-right corner.

Font icon

The first icon on the second toolbar is the Font icon. Tap the Font icon to access the following useful features:

- ✔ **Fonts:** Change the font size and the typeface by tapping the options in the first section shown in Figure 3-5.

- ✔ **Line spacing:** Tap the boxes to choose tight, average, or wide line spacing.

✔ **Margins:** Tap the boxes to change the width of the page margin to wide, average, or narrow.

Close the menu by tapping the X in the upper-right corner.

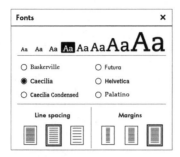

Figure 3-5: Tap the Font icon to change the appearance of text on the screen.

Go To

Tap Go To to display a two-tabbed menu that allows you to quickly navigate through a book and your notes. The Contents tab displays information such as Cover, Book Info, Beginning (the first page of the first chapter), Table of Contents (from here, you can tap and move to individual chapters), End (the last location in the book), and a specific page or location. The Notes tab displays your notes as public notes from other readers. Navigating through a book using the Go To feature is discussed in more detail in Chapter 4.

X-Ray

Tap X-Ray to display a list of words or characters that appear in the page, chapter, or book, along with a frequency graph. (For details on the X-ray feature, see Chapter 8.) X-Ray appears dimmed if the feature is not enabled in the book you're reading.

Share

Tap Share to open a screen that allows you to type comments about the book you're reading. Comments will be shared to Goodreads as well as to Twitter and Facebook, if they are selected. You must have your social networks enabled and connected to your Kindle Paperwhite to be able to use this feature. (See Chapter 8 for details.)

Bookmark icon

Tapping the Bookmark icon allows you to quickly place a bookmark at the location you're reading, to save your place or for future reference. Setting a bookmark and using bookmarks to navigate are discussed in detail in Chapter 4.

Toolbars when viewing periodicals

Within a periodical, such as a newspaper or a magazine, the toolbars are a little different. The main toolbar still contains Home, Back, Light, Search, and Menu icons, but the Store icon is replaced by the following two icons:

- ✔ **Cover view icon:** Tap this icon to see the list of sections with photographs, as shown in Figure 3-6.

Figure 3-6: Cover view of the *New York Times.*

✔ **Section view icon:** This icon displays a hierarchical, text-based section and article listing, as shown in Figure 3-7. At the bottom of the screen are navigation arrows.

The Back icon returns you to the article listing or the front page. Newspaper and magazine content is sorted by lists of articles or sections that you scroll through to select what you want to read. For tips on reading periodicals, see Chapter 4.

The second toolbar that you see when reading an article in a periodical (such as a magazine or newspaper) is different than the one you see when reading a book. Both toolbars sport the Font icon. But instead of Go To, X-Ray, and Share, which you see when reading a book, you see Clip This Article, as shown in Figure 3-8. Tapping Clip This Article to quickly add an article of interest to the My Clippings file. (For details, see Chapter 4.)

Dec 3, 2013	Kindle Edition, © 2013 The New York Times Company
Sections	**Articles**
Front Page	Metro-North Train Sped at 82 M.P.H. Into 30 M.P.H. Zone Before Crash
International	
National	Seeing the Toll, Schools Revise Zero Tolerance
Editorials, Op-Ed and...	As Hospital Prices Soar, a Single Stitch Tops $500
Business Day	A New Wave of Challenges to Health Law
Sports Tuesday	Kurds' Oil Deals With Turkey Raise Fears of Fissures in Iraq
The Arts	
Science Times	Fates of Brooks and Coulson in Tabloid Hacking Case Are Diverging
Corrections	
Most E-Mailed	
∧ 1 - 10 of 12 ∨	∧ 1 - 6 of 6 ∨

Figure 3-7: Section view of the *New York Times.*

Figure 3-8: You see the second toolbar when reading a periodical.

Navigating with Page Flip

Page Flip on the Kindle Paperwhite enables you to move quickly through a book and return to your original location, without setting a bookmark. To access Page Flip, swipe up from the bottom of the screen. You'll see a screen within the screen, as shown in Figure 3-9.

In the middle of the page, note the left and right arrowheads. Tap these to move forward (right) or backward (left) one page at a time. You can move forward and backward through a book also by swiping across the screen.

At the bottom of the screen is a rectangular navigation pane that displays the current chapter and location. Tap the arrows to move forward and backward by chapter. (If the publisher hasn't set chapter marks, you see only the progress bar.) You can slide the circle on the progress bar to move forward quickly by location — think of this as riffling through the book. Tap on the bar to move to the beginning of a chapter. When you're finished, tap the X in the upper-right corner to close Page Flip and return to your reading location.

Page Flip is a handy feature because it allows you to quickly move through a book without losing your place. Do you need to refresh your memory on a character's name? Does the book contain maps or photographs? Use Page Flip to navigate to these types of features.

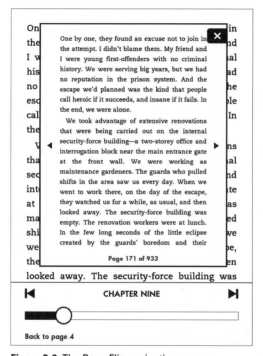

Figure 3-9: The Page Flip navigation screen.

You can use Page Flip to quickly jump to a different part of the book (if, for example, you've lost your place and didn't set a bookmark). After you've flipped to the correct location, tap the center of the page view screen to jump to that location.

The size of the font in the page view screen is smaller than the font on the page you're reading. If the Page Flip view is too small to read, increase the size of the font on the page and then restart Page Flip. You can't directly increase the font size within the inserted page that you're viewing on the screen.

Chapter 4

Reading

. . . .

In This Chapter

▶ Understanding your Kindle Paperwhite's basic reading features

▶ Viewing and sorting content on your device and in the Cloud

▶ Reading a periodical efficiently

▶ Making the most of comic books, graphic novels, and manga

▶ Organizing your content in collections

▶ Reading on other devices

. . . .

*I*n this chapter, I show you the basics of reading on your Kindle Paperwhite — a process so simple and elegant that you'll soon forget you're even using an e-reader.

You also find out how to navigate through your collection of books both on your Kindle Paperwhite and in the Cloud. In addition, I include information on how to have a stellar experience when reading periodicals, such as newspapers and magazines. Along the way, I share tips and hints that can save you time and make the most of your reading experience.

It All Begins on the Home Screen

The Home screen displays a list of all the content loaded on your Kindle Paperwhite. Typically, that content is mostly books but can also include games, newspapers, magazines, blogs, and personal documents.

When you turn on your Kindle Paperwhite (by pressing the power button on the bottom edge or opening the cover if the device is in an Amazon case), it displays your last viewed page or a sponsored screensaver, which you swipe to get to the last viewed screen (if you're using a Kindle Paperwhite with special offers). You can always go directly to your Home screen by tapping the Home icon on the toolbar at the top of the screen. If the toolbar is not displayed, just tap in the top half-inch of the screen and it will appear.

If you're using the Amazon cover, your Kindle Paperwhite will automatically come out of Sleep mode when you open the cover. If you have a Kindle Paperwhite with traditional screensavers, you'll see the last viewed screen. A Kindle Paperwhite with special offers and sponsored screensavers will display one of those screens. Give the screen a quick swipe to display the last viewed screen.

Figure 4-1 shows a typical Home screen on a Kindle Paperwhite.

Figure 4-1: The Home screen in List view.

The Home screen on the Kindle Paperwhite with special offers and sponsored screensavers displays seven items — one slot for content is taken up by the small special offer banner at the bottom of the screen. If you don't have special offers on your Kindle Paperwhite, eight items will be listed.

The Home screen in Figure 4-1 is shown in List view. If you prefer, you can view your Home screen in Cover view, which is shown in Figure 4-2.

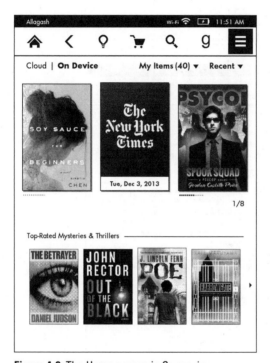

Figure 4-2: The Home screen in Cover view.

If you've selected By Author or By Title on the Home screen, the first page of Cover view displays three covers of your content and four covers of something Amazon thinks you might enjoy (top-rated mysteries and thrillers in Figure 4-2). When you tap to move to the next page, the Home screen will display six covers generated from your content. If you're viewing your Home screen By Collection, generic covers for the collections will be shown. The generic collection covers will be mixed in as appropriate in the other views.

Perhaps you don't like seeing Amazon's recommendations and would prefer to see six covers of your content on every screen. No problem — you have the option to change the display. Tap Menu⇨Settings⇨Device Options⇨Personalize Your Kindle. Recommended content is an on/off toggle switch, as shown in Figure 4-3.

When you turn off Recommended Content, the screen will display six covers, as shown in Figure 4-4.

To switch from List view to Cover view, simply tap Menu⇨Cover View. To switch back, tap Menu⇨List View.

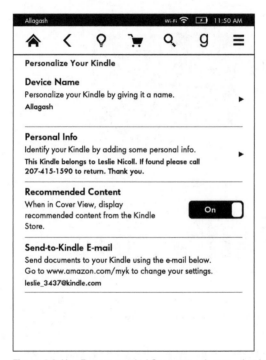

Figure 4-3: Use Recommended Content to choose what is displayed in Cover view.

Figure 4-4: Cover display with Recommended Content turned off.

Types of Content

I would hazard a guess that if I picked up a stranger's Kindle Paperwhite, the most common type of content on the device I would see would be books. But that's not the only type of material that you can read, as you can see from the following list:

- ✔ **Books:** Every type of book, from traditional novels to short stories, serialized books, Kindle Singles, and more.

- ✔ **Periodicals:** Newspapers, magazines, and blogs.

- ✔ **Docs:** Personal documents that you create and send to your Kindle whether using Send to Kindle or e-mail (see Chapter 7 for details on this process). In addition, if you capture content from the web and send it to your Kindle Paperwhite by using the Send to Kindle browser feature, this material will be categorized as a Doc.

- ✔ **Active Content:** Games such as "Every Word."

Throughout this book, when I refer to *content,* I mean any of the preceding categories.

Moving around the Home Screen

When you first get your Kindle Paperwhite, you may have only one page of content listed on your Home screen. You can easily open a book from the list by tapping anywhere on its name. As the amount of content on your device grows, however, you'll want to be able to move around quickly and easily.

How do you know how many pages of content you have on your Home screen? Look at the bottom-right corner in Figures 4-1 and 4-4. Note the two numbers separated by a slash. The first number is the page you're on; the second number is the total number of pages of content. For convenience, I refer to these numbers as the *page indicator.*

As you add books and other content, your Home screen can quickly become many pages long. After all, your Kindle Paperwhite can hold about 1,100 e-books! You'll probably accumulate books quickly, given the availability of free material and the ease with which you can download content.

What's more, if you get in the habit of sampling books before you buy, your library of content can really start to mushroom! (I discuss sampling in Chapter 5.)

So how do you manage your fast-growing library? The following sections describe features available from your Home screen that help you browse through your library and find books efficiently.

Sorting and displaying content

The top-right corner of the Home screen provides four options for sorting content: Recent, Title, Author, and Collections. To change the current sort method, simply tap it and then tap your new choice. *Presto!* Your list appears, re-sorted.

The Recent option displays the most recent content either loaded or viewed on your Kindle Paperwhite. Title, Author, and Collections are displayed alphabetically. When sorted by Collections, the collections appear first and books not in collections appear next, sorted by most recent. If you haven't set up any collections, the Collections choice appears dimmed on the menu. I discuss how to organize your content into collections in the "Creating Collections" section, later in this chapter.

You can also restrict the type of content shown on your Kindle Paperwhite by tapping the down arrow next to My Items. (By default, the device displays My Items, which displays every type of item on your device, with the total number of items listed in parentheses.) Tap Books, Periodicals, Docs, and Active Content (see the "Types of Content" section) to display content only in those categories. The number in parentheses will change depending on the number of items on your Kindle Paperwhite in that particular category.

Removing content

Although it's great to keep adding books and other content to your Kindle Paperwhite, sometimes you'll want to remove items — whether to save space or because you don't like clutter. Some Kindle users don't like to re-read books, so they have no reason to keep books they've read on their device. Whatever the case, realize that sometimes removing content is permanent.

If you long-tap a book's title, you will see that Remove from Device is the last choice on the menu that appears. If you purchased the book from Amazon, it will be available in the Cloud, which is your archive of Kindle books at Amazon. If you remove the book from the device, it is still available to you to download via the Cloud.

However, if you have purchased a book from another source, it will not be backed up in the Cloud, unless you have sent it to your device by using one of the options described in Chapter 7. In this case, when you remove the book, it is permanently deleted unless you have backed it up on your computer.

Unfortunately, the menu doesn't indicate whether the removal is permanent — you need to remember where you acquired the material.

If you long-tap the title of a sample, you'll see the Delete This Sample option at the bottom of the list. Deleting a sample is permanent, although you can always download the sample again from Amazon.

Paging through the Home screen

If your Home screen has multiple pages, you can flip forward and backward through those pages by swiping from right to left (to move forward) or left to right (to move backward). Note that this swipe can be horizontal or diagonal in List and Cover views, as well as vertical (up to move forward, down to go back) in List view.

From the Home screen, you can navigate directly to a page in your list of books. Begin by tapping the page indicator at the bottom-right corner of the screen. A pop-up window appears, allowing you to enter a page number to jump directly to the list of content. If your Home screen is sorted by Collections, Recent, or Title, you'll also have the option of entering the first few letters of a book's title. If your Home screen is sorted by Author, you can enter the first letters of an author's name. Tap the Go button and you're taken to the corresponding page in your list of content.

Searching from the Home screen

Another way to find a book is to use the device's powerful Search feature, which can scan all your content to find items containing a word or string of characters.

To search from the Home screen, tap the Search icon on the toolbar. The Search screen and onscreen keyboard appear, as shown in Figure 4-5.

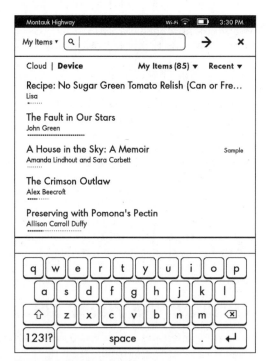

Figure 4-5: The Search screen.

When using the onscreen keyboard, you can access variations of certain letters by tapping and holding down on a letter. For example, tapping and holding down on the letter E displays accent marks and other diacriticals. Enter text by tapping the appropriate letters on the keyboard, and then tap the arrow to the right of the search box.

The search feature is powerful, and you need to set the parameters carefully to make sure you get the results you want. When you bring up the search bar, look to the left to see what is displayed. If it says My Items, your search will return titles and author names that match your search item in content that is on your Kindle Paperwhite as well as in the Cloud (your archive) at Amazon. Alternatively, if you select All Text, the search will be restricted to content on your Kindle Paperwhite, but it will search all the text on your Paperwhite, not just titles and author names.

Figure 4-6 shows the results of a search for *bride* with My Items selected. Figure 4-7 shows the same search with All Text as the selected parameter.

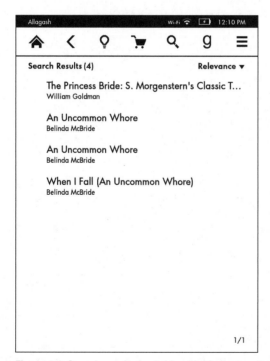

Figure 4-6: Search results for *bride* with My Items selected.

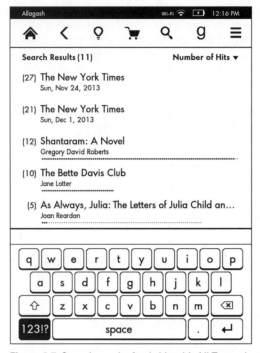

Figure 4-7: Search results for *bride* with All Text selected.

The number in parentheses next to a title indicates the number of occurrences, or *hits,* of the search term. For content on your Kindle Paperwhite (All Text parameter), your search results are sorted by number of hits by default. Higher relevance is given to books with the search word in the title or with many occurrences of the word in the text.

You can change the order in which your search options are displayed. At the top of the screen, tap the down arrow next to Number of Hits to see the other sort options: Recent (sorts by the most recent items loaded on the device or viewed), Title (sorts alphabetically), and Author (sorts alphabetically).

When you load new content on your Kindle Paperwhite, the device automatically indexes it — which is why the search function works. Occasionally, though, a file is indexed incorrectly. When this happens, you see *Unindexed Items* at the end of the search retrieval list. Unindexed items can quickly drain the battery. See Chapter 11 for troubleshooting hints to correct this problem.

Tap on the title of one of the retrieved (searched) items to display the results screen. A page highlights the search term in context, with the location number and, if applicable, the page number in the book.

Tap the paragraph to go directly to the page in the book (or other content) that contains your search term. To go back to the search results, display the top menu and tap the Back icon twice.

Selecting a book to read

Any of the methods discussed in the previous sections can be used to quickly find books from your Home screen. When you find the book you want to read, simply tap the displayed title to open it. (If the book is in the Cloud, tap the title to download it and then tap it again to open it.)

Viewing content in the Cloud

If you purchase books, magazines, newspapers, or games from Amazon, those items are stored in the Cloud at your account. To view content in the Cloud as well as on your device, tap Cloud in the top left of the screen. When you do so, the number next to My Items changes to reflect the number of items stored in the Cloud. Items that are in the Cloud and on your device display a check mark, as shown in Figure 4-8.

Before the introduction of the Kindle Paperwhite, the Cloud was known as Archived Items.

You sort and view content in the Cloud the way you do on your device. Tap the arrow next to My Items to select All Items, Books, Periodicals, Docs, and Active Content. You can also sort items by Recent, Title, and Author.

To download content to your Kindle Paperwhite, tap its title. Your wireless connection (Wi-Fi or 3G) must be turned on. If wireless is not turned on — which means your device is in Airplane mode — you'll be asked if you want to turn off Airplane mode.

You can view items in the Cloud without a wireless connection, but Wi-Fi or 3G must be on to download content.

Only content purchased from Amazon is automatically available for viewing in the Cloud. If you've bought or downloaded books from other sites and you want to have that material stored in the Cloud, you need to move it there. The easiest way to do so is to use Send to Kindle, which is discussed in Chapter 7.

If you want to use a computer to view your content in the Cloud, go directly to your Kindle Library at www.amazon.com/myk.

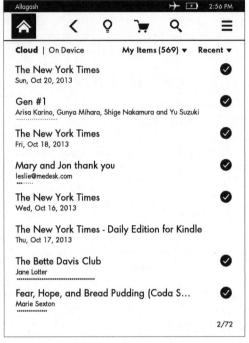

Figure 4-8: The check marks indicate that content is in the Cloud and on the Kindle Paperwhite.

Moving through a Book

Reading a book on a Kindle Paperwhite is intuitive. To go to the next page, tap anywhere on the page, except near the top and along the left. (See Chapter 3 for illustrations of the tap zones in Portrait and Landscape modes.) Tap near the left edge of the display to move back one page. To see the toolbar, tap near the top edge of the display.

As noted previously, you can also swipe left or right to page forward and backward, respectively. Page Flip (discussed in Chapter 3) is another way to move quickly through a book.

Going to a specific spot

You can also jump directly to various parts of a book. Tap near the top of the screen to display the toolbars, and then tap Go To. A pop-up menu appears, as shown in Figure 4-9.

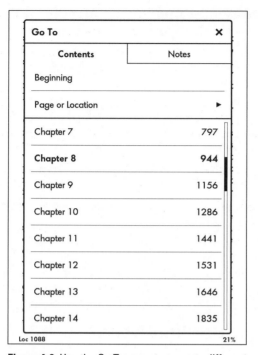

Figure 4-9: Use the Go To menu to move to different sections of a book.

Note the two tabs at the top of the menu that display Contents and Notes. You use the Contents tab to navigate through the book, and the Notes tab to navigate through personal annotations you've made, as well as popular and public annotations.

 To see popular and public annotations on the Notes section of the Go To screen, you must have Popular Highlights and Public Notes enabled. To turn them on, tap Menu⇨Settings⇨Reading Options⇨Notes & Highlights. Use the toggle switch to turn on Popular Highlights and Public Notes.

When the Contents tab is selected, the list of Go To options may differ depending on the book. Here are the options you may see:

✓ **Beginning:** The first words of text in the book.

✓ **Page or Location:** A particular page or location in the book. I discuss the concept of *page* and *location* as they pertain to e-books shortly.

✓ **Cover:** The book's cover.

✔ **Book Info or Front Matter:** Content that appears before the start of the book, such as a dedication and copyright page.

✔ **Chapter listing:** The list of chapters, similar to a traditional table of contents. Tap a chapter title or number to go directly to that chapter.

If the chapter listing is more than one page long, swipe up the list with your finger to advance to additional chapters. A scroll bar indicator on the right provides an approximation of the length of the list (refer to Figure 4-9).

✔ **About the Author:** Biographical information about the author of the book.

✔ **Recommended Reads:** A list of additional books by the same publisher or author.

✔ **End:** The end of the book, which displays a page where you can rate and share the book on Amazon and Goodreads. If your Kindle Paperwhite is linked to Facebook through Goodreads, your rating will also be posted to this social networking site.

Setting a bookmark

You can use personal bookmarks to help you navigate through a book. To set a bookmark, tap in the upper-right corner of the screen. A flag appears, along with the location and chapter (or part) of the book, with a plus sign (+) in a circle. To set the bookmark, simply tap the plus sign. The flag darkens, indicating the marked location.

After you set a bookmark, tap the upper-right corner and a small menu appears, displaying *all* the bookmarks that have been set in the book. When you tap a bookmarked location, a window insert opens on the screen, as shown in Figure 4-10. You can read the page from the insert or go directly to it by tapping the page on the screen. To return to your former location, navigate by bookmark or use the Back icon from the toolbar.

To delete a bookmark, tap the X in the drop-down menu. To add the bookmark again, tap +. Note that the display toggles between + and X, depending on whether or not a bookmark is set.

Finding your place

The Kindle Paperwhite gives you several options for knowing your location in a book.

Figure 4-10: The navigation screen from a bookmarked location.

As you read, the area at the bottom of the screen displays a location number for the text currently in view and a percentage indicating how much of the book you've read. Tap the location number to cycle through the minutes left in the chapter, the hours and minutes left in the book, the location, and when available, the page number. Your final choice becomes the default.

All e-books have location information, but not all have page numbers. (For example, if a book exists only in e-book form, page numbers are not available.) Time to dig into the difference in these terms and how you may use them to reference different parts of a book:

✔ **Location:** The concept of a fixed, printed page doesn't apply to e-books because you can vary the font type, font size, line spacing, and words per line. These changes affect how much of the e-book is displayed on a given screen. Instead of page numbers, *location* is used as a marker to indicate how far you are in an e-book. The location remains constant even if the screen or font size changes.

One unit of location is equivalent to 128 bytes of information in the e-book file.

✔ **Page number:** Many e-books can also display a page number that reflects the page number in the printed edition of the book. This information is helpful, for example, if you're in a reading group in which some members use Kindles and others use printed copies of the book.

For e-books that display page numbers, you may be curious as to which version of the printed book matches those page numbers. You can find this out by going to the e-book's product details on Amazon and opening the drop-down menu next to the page number listing. The ISBN for the book that served as the source for the page numbers is displayed, as shown in Figure 4-11.

Figure 4-11: Determining the source for page numbers in a Kindle e-book.

Discovering your reading speed

The Kindle Paperwhite can learn your reading speed, so it can tell you how many minutes or hours of reading time remain in the current chapter or book.

How does the Kindle Paperwhite determine how much reading time is left in a chapter or book? When you first open a book, *Learning reading speed* appears at the bottom of the screen. After the device calculates your reading speed, it uses this figure for the rest of your reading experience in that particular document.

The device can relearn your reading speed. This feature is helpful if you've paged quickly through a book, making the reading speed inaccurate. Simply tap the top of the screen to display the toolbar, touch the Search icon (see the margin), and type the following:

```
;ReadingTimeReset
```

Tap the search arrow and the device will display *0 search results.* Tap the Back icon and *Learning reading speed* will again be displayed at the bottom of the screen.

Menu options for books

When reading a book, you can access useful features by tapping the top of the screen to display the toolbar and then tapping the Menu icon. The following options appear:

- ✔ **Shop Kindle Store:** Go to the Kindle Store to browse and find e-books.

- ✔ **Vocabulary Builder:** Open the list of words you have looked up in the dictionary.

- ✔ **Settings:** Toggle Airplane mode on and off and access options for Wi-Fi networks, registration, reading, parental controls, time, language, and more.

- ✔ **Book Description:** Display the book's Kindle Store description. Wireless must be on (that is, Airplane mode must be off) to view this information.

- ✔ **About the Author:** When available, see biographical information about the author as well as a list of other Kindle books that the author has written.

- ✔ **Landscape Mode:** Change the orientation of the page from Portrait to Landscape mode.

In Landscape mode, you need to tap the top of the page (which would normally be the left side of the screen) to display the toolbar.

- ✔ **Sync to Furthest Page Read:** If you (or others on your Amazon account) have viewed the current book on another device, you can adjust your location to the furthest page read. To reset the furthest page read (for example, if you want to re-read the book, or if someone else on your account has already read the book), go to the book's listing in Manage Your Kindle and select Clear Furthest Page Read in the drop-down menu on the right.

Select this option if you want to use Whispersync to synchronize your Kindle Paperwhite book with an audiobook from Audible. Audiobooks and Whispersync are described in Chapter 8.

- ✔ **Reading Progress:** Select the default for the reading progress displayed at the bottom of the screen (location in book, time left in chapter, or time left in book).

You can reset the default location also by simply toggling through the choices at the bottom of the screen.

Reading Newspapers and Magazines

Books are typically organized into chapters, which are read in a linear fashion, that is, from beginning to end. Periodicals such as newspapers and magazines, on the other hand, usually contain a number of articles grouped by section. Readers often choose to skip around among sections and articles. Fortunately, the Kindle Paperwhite has several special features to enhance the experience of reading periodicals.

Basic navigation

From the Home screen, tap the title of the periodical you want to read. By default, it opens in a view that displays different sections, with the number of articles in each section. For example, Figure 4-12 shows the default display from a recent issue of *Reader's Digest*.

Figure 4-12: The default Cover view of a periodical.

Tap the top of the screen to display the toolbar. The Store icon you see while reading a book has been replaced by two icons that enable you to switch between the default Cover view and the Section view. You can think of these views as similar to Cover view and List view on the Home screen (see the "Moving around the Home screen" section, earlier in this chapter).

Figure 4-13 illustrates the Section view of the Sports Friday section of the *New York Times*. The left side of the screen lists the various sections, and the right side lists the articles in the selected section. The bottom left shows the total number of sections (11) and the bottom right displays the total number of articles (20). Tap the section or article you want to read.

You can navigate through the pages of sections and articles by using the arrows at the bottom of the screen or by simply swiping the screen.

You can move forward in a periodical in a linear fashion by tapping the title of the next article at the bottom of the screen. The percentage that appears to the left of this navigation bar shows how far in the article you've read.

Figure 4-13: The Section view of a periodical.

Menu options for periodicals

 When you tap the Menu icon while reading a periodical, you see fewer options than those for a book:

- ✔ **Shop Kindle Store:** Go to the Kindle Store to browse and find periodicals and e-books.

- ✔ **Vocabulary Builder:** Open the list of words you have looked up in the dictionary.

- ✔ **Settings:** Toggle Airplane mode on and off and access options for Wi-Fi networks, registration, reading, parental controls, time, language, and more.

- ✔ **Keep This Issue:** Store the periodical on your device until you choose to remove it. (When a periodical has already been stored, the option changes to Do Not Keep This Issue.)

- ✔ **Sync to Furthest Page Read:** If you (or others on your Amazon account) have viewed the periodical on another device, you can adjust your location to the furthest page read. If no one else has read this periodical, the choice will appear dimmed.

- ✔ **View Notes & Marks:** Display the highlighted sections, notes, and bookmarks for the current periodical.

- ✔ **Share:** Share articles of interest on Facebook and Twitter. See Chapter 8 for more information on using these social media sites to share favorite content with your friends.

In addition, the second toolbar sports a Clip This Article option. Tap that option to save an article to your My Clippings file. My Clippings is listed on your Home screen, just like a book or other content. If My Clippings isn't at the top of the list, swipe through the pages — it's probably at the end.

Reading Comic Books and Manga

Do you enjoy graphic novels, comics, and manga? You can read all these on your Kindle Paperwhite. A few special features improve the reading experience for these visual documents.

- ✔ **Panel view:** In a book with multiple panels on a page, you can double-tap the screen to enlarge each panel to full-screen for an optimized reading experience. In this Panel view, simply tap the screen to advance through each panel individually (see Figure 4-14). When you reach the last panel (the equivalent of reading one page in the print version), the screen displays the next page of panels, and then displays each panel separately as you tap. In this way, you can see the "big picture" but also read each panel easily. Double-tap to exit Panel view.

✔ **Refresh every page:** You can set the screen refresh to refresh every page in a comic, graphic novel, or manga — independent of the setting you have for other books on your device. Tap Menu⇨Page Refresh On. The menu will display Page Refresh On (as shown in Figure 4-15) or Page Refresh Off, depending on what you have selected.

If the Page Refresh On option doesn't appear on the menu, the book has probably not been configured to take advantage of this feature.

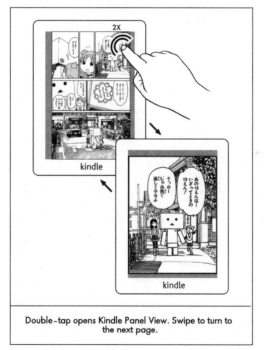

Double-tap opens Kindle Panel View. Swipe to turn to the next page.

Figure 4-14: This manga provides instructions on how to change to single-panel view.

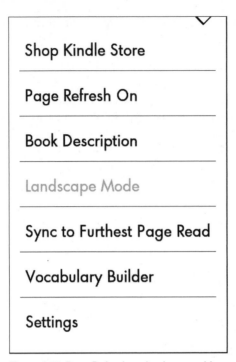

Shop Kindle Store

Page Refresh On

Book Description

Landscape Mode

Sync to Furthest Page Read

Vocabulary Builder

Settings

Figure 4-15: Page Refresh option in a graphic novel or manga.

Creating Collections

As you use your Kindle Paperwhite, you'll likely deal with a long and growing list of e-books and other content on the device, and putting your fingers on specific content can become challenging.

You can organize this cornucopia of content with collections. For example, if you want to keep track of all books you've read in a given year, you could create a Finished in 2013 collection. You might want to put dictionaries and product manuals in a References collection. (Note that a Dictionaries collection is automatically created for you; it appears at the end of your list of content.) Perhaps you want to set up collections for your favorite genres: Paranormal, Romance, Horror, Biographies, and so on.

For some clever titles for collections, see the list in Chapter 12.

Note that periodical back issues are stored in their own collection, following the Dictionaries collection in your list of content. You can't create a collection containing both periodicals and books.

To create a collection, follow these steps:

1. **From the Home screen, tap the Menu icon.**
2. **Tap Create New Collection.**

   A pop-up window appears.

3. **Using the onscreen keyboard, enter a name for the new collection.**

   A list of your content appears, both on your Kindle Paperwhite and in the Cloud.

4. **Tap the check box for each title you want to add to the collection.**
5. **When you're finished, tap Done.**

   The collection is created.

You can add books after you've created a collection, as follows:

1. **From the Home screen, tap and briefly hold down on the name of the e-book.**

   A set of options appears.

2. **Tap Add to Collection.**
3. **Tap the check box for the collection to which you want to add the book.**
4. **Tap Done.**

You can assign a book to more than one collection. For example, you might put a book in a Finished collection as well as a Biographies collection.

After you move your book to a collection, you might be surprised to see it appear on your Home screen list. When you sort the Home screen by title, collections are listed alphabetically along with all the books on your Kindle Paperwhite. If you instead sort the Home screen by collections, your collections are displayed in alphabetical order, followed by any books and other content that aren't assigned to a collection. (See the "Sorting and displaying content" section, earlier in this chapter, for details on sorting your content.)

When you view a collection, books on your Kindle Paperwhite are displayed in dark letters with a check mark in the right column. Items in the Cloud appear dimmed. If you tap a dimmed title, the book will be downloaded to your Kindle Paperwhite, assuming wireless is turned on and your Kindle Paperwhite is connected.

If it is in Airplane mode, a message appears asking if you want to turn off Airplane mode. Tap OK and the item will automatically download from the Cloud to your Kindle.

You can change to Cover view from within a collection. Tap Menu Menu⇨Cover View.

To remove items from a collection or to delete a collection, open the collection and tap the Menu icon. You see options to Add/Remove Items, Rename Collection, and Delete Collection. Note that if you delete a collection, any books contained in the collection are not deleted from your Kindle Paperwhite. You can delete a collection also by long-tapping the collection name on the Home screen.

Reading on Other Devices

E-books purchased from the Kindle Store can be read not only on your Kindle Paperwhite but also on the following devices, when used with a free Kindle reading app:

- PC
- Mac
- iPad, iPhone, and iPod touch
- Kindle Cloud Reader
- Android tablet
- Android phone
- Windows phone
- Kindle for Windows 8
- BlackBerry 10
- WebOS

The list of supported devices is likely to grow over time. For a current list of supported devices, go to the Kindle Support page (www.amazon.com/gp/help/customer/display.html) and choose Kindle Help⇨Kindle Reading Applications.

To read Kindle e-books on other devices, you need to install the free reading app and register those devices to your account. The registration process should happen automatically, but you can also register from your Manage Your Kindle page (www.amazon.com/myk). You're prompted to sign in if you haven't already done so. Tap the Manage Your Devices link, and then scroll down to the Registered Kindle Reading App section for instructions for your particular device.

You can use Whispersync to keep your reading synchro-
nized across all devices registered to your Amazon account.
Whispersync synchronizes the furthest page read as well as your
bookmarks, notes, and highlights. Remember that for the synchronization to take place, wireless must be turned on in each of the
devices to be synced.

Whispersync for Voice allows you to sync between a Kindle edition
of an e-book and an audio version from Audible.com. See Chapter 8
for details.

If you want to turn off Whispersync, go to the Manage Your Kindle
page on Amazon (www.amazon.com/myk) and then tap Manage
Your Devices. The Device Synchronization area provides a link
where you can turn synchronization on and off.

Chapter 5

Finding Content

In This Chapter

▶ Searching in the Kindle Store

▶ Exploring other online stores

▶ Finding free content resources

You're holding your Kindle Paperwhite in your hand — it's registered, charged, and ready to go. What do you want to do? Read, of course! But to make that happen, you need to have content on your Kindle Paperwhite. Although the way the wireless service downloads content to your Kindle Paperwhite seems almost magical, you need to initiate the process. This chapter discusses finding content — from books to blogs and everything in between — and how to get the treasures you find onto your Kindle Paperwhite in the easiest way possible.

Starting Your Search in the Kindle Store

The fastest, easiest, and most convenient place to find Kindle Paperwhite content is at the Amazon Kindle Store, which makes sense because Amazon invented the device.

One common misconception is that you have to buy *all* Kindle content from Amazon. This isn't true. Although Amazon makes shopping for Kindle Paperwhite content simple, you can find plenty of other online stores that sell Kindle-compatible e-books, as discussed later in this chapter in the "Checking Out Other Online Stores" section.

Searching and browsing on your computer

Amazon has a specific Kindle Store that makes it easy to search for Kindle Paperwhite content. Using your computer, go to www. amazon.com. From the Search drop-down list, choose Kindle Store to restrict your search to Kindle-specific content, as shown in Figure 5-1.

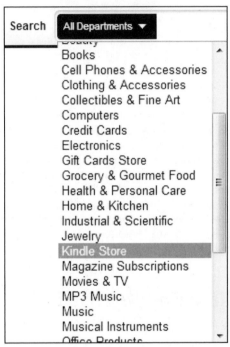

Figure 5-1: Restricting your search to the Kindle Store.

In the Search field, type the words for your search. Do you have a specific book in mind? Type a few words of the title. Are you looking for books by a particular author? Type the author's name. Are you interested in deep-sea diving — or any other subject that tickles your fancy? Type a few words, click the Go button to the right of the Search field, and voilà! If anything on the topic is in the store, it appears in the search results. With millions of Kindle-compatible e-books in the store and 180,000 exclusive Kindle titles (as of this writing), something will probably appear!

Just for fun, I entered **archery** and received an interesting assortment of results (416 in all): a variety of non-fiction e-books including a history of bows and arrows; how to make a crossbow; how to *fletch* (or put feathers on) arrows; the Zen of archery; Kyudo, the Japanese art of archery; a business plan for an archery store; and novels such as *The Last Elf of Lanis* by K. J. Hargan. Several other books were also available for loan through the Kindle Owners' Lending Library. (See Chapter 6 for more about borrowing books through this program.)

If you're more of a browser and less of a searcher, Amazon makes that easy, too. After you choose the Kindle Store and tap Go, a bar appears below the search bar, listing the departments in the Kindle Store:

- ✔ Buy a Kindle
- ✔ Kindle eBooks
- ✔ Advanced Search
- ✔ Daily Deals
- ✔ Free Reading Apps
- ✔ Kindle Singles
- ✔ Newsstand
- ✔ Accessories
- ✔ Discussions
- ✔ Manage Your Kindle
- ✔ Kindle Support

One frequently asked question at KBoards.com is "How do I contact Kindle support?" Just click the Kindle Support link, as shown in Figure 5-2.

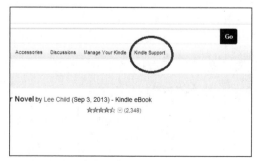

Figure 5-2: Click the Kindle Support link to find help.

Click the Kindle eBooks link, and you land on a page that should happily satisfy your browsing dreams. In the center of the page are lists such as Kindle Select 25, which features 25 noteworthy books for the week, New & Noteworthy Kindle Books, Picks for You, and other options (note that this page changes frequently) with the book covers prominently featured.

The left side of the page includes multiple categories to start your search, with Kindle Book Deals at the top of the list. Here you'll find Kindle Daily Deals, Monthly Deals ($3.99 or less), and the Big Deal — up to 80 percent off more than 350 books. The next category, Popular Features, includes Kindle Best Sellers, *The New York Times* Best Sellers, and Editor's Picks. Third on the list are categories for searching specific topic areas, so you can drill down a bit more while browsing. Gay & Lesbian? Travel? Click the link, and you're presented with a plethora of choices to capture your fancy. The last four categories are More to Explore, Newsstand, Kindle Gifts, and a link to obtain help.

The right side of the page shows a number of lists that are updated hourly, including the Top 100 Paid and Top 100 Free. Kindle Daily Deals are featured prominently at the top of the screen, along with a button to allow you to subscribe so you never miss a single deal.

Even though over a million Kindle-compatible e-books are in the Kindle Store, millions upon millions of printed books are in the world. Unfortunately, they aren't all available in a Kindle edition. If a particular book you want is for sale at Amazon (U.S.) in print form but not in a Kindle edition, click the Tell the Publisher! I'd Like to Read This Book on Kindle link on the book's product page. Does clicking the link make a difference? I suspect that it does. For example, popular author J. K. Rowling was originally opposed to e-books, but the Harry Potter series became available as e-books in 2012. The Potter books are available also to borrow for free through the Kindle Owners' Lending Library. Consumer demand likely influenced these changes.

Searching and browsing on your Kindle Paperwhite

"Wait a minute!" I hear you saying, "I don't want to use my computer to search for e-books. Can I search from my Kindle Paperwhite?" Of course you can! Simply tap the Store icon on the toolbar. If the wireless is not turned on, you will receive a message to take your Kindle Paperwhite out of Airplane mode, as shown in Figure 5-3.

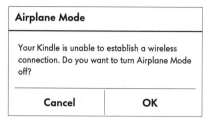

Airplane Mode

Your Kindle is unable to establish a wireless connection. Do you want to turn Airplane Mode off?

| Cancel | OK |

Figure 5-3: Turn off Airplane mode to connect wirelessly.

If you have a Wi-Fi–only Kindle Paperwhite, you need to be somewhere with a Wi-Fi hotspot. If you have a Kindle Paperwhite 3G, you should be good to go anywhere that has 3G service.

When the wireless is on and has a good connection, tap the Shop in Kindle Store icon (see the margin) or tap the Menu icon (also in the margin) and select Shop in Kindle Store from the drop-down menu that appears. Either way, you see a page similar to the one shown in Figure 5-4 when you connect to the Kindle Store.

Figure 5-4: Browse for e-books and more from your Kindle Paperwhite.

At the top of the screen, you have the option to browse Books, Newspapers, Kindles Singles, Kindle Serials, Kindle Worlds, and Magazines. As you move down the page, you can browse the Daily Deals, Monthly Deals, Best Sellers, Kindle Select 25, Best of the Month, Things to Try, and New & Noteworthy. At the time this screenshot was taken, the list also featured 2013 Pulitzer Winners.

The bottom panel changes frequently. In Figure 5-4, it displays the Best of 2013. Other times, the bottom panel might feature Recommended for You, which are books that might be of interest to you based on your purchases. The more you buy from Amazon, the more tailored the recommendations are to your interests.

At the top of the screen is a Search field so that you can search the store, just as you do from your computer. Tapping in the Search field displays the onscreen keyboard. Type an author's name, the title of a book, or a search term.

To exit the store and return to the Home screen, tap the Home icon or the Back icon.

Sampling content

When you find a book that intrigues you, you can send a sample to your Kindle Paperwhite to decide whether you really want to purchase it. *Samples* consist of the first 10 percent of the book, which is usually enough to give you a flavor of the writing. Sampling isn't perfect, however; sometimes the first 10 percent of a book is mostly the *front matter* (the table of contents, foreword, acknowledgments, and so on), and you never get to the good stuff. However, based on my experience, this problem occurs less frequently than it did in the early days of Kindle e-books. Publishers seem to be aware of the issue and are formatting their e-books so that relevant content is included in the sample, allowing a potential buyer to make an informed purchase decision.

If you enjoy the sample and want to buy the book, you can do so in a number of ways. The easiest method is to tap the top of the screen to display not only the top toolbar but also a special bottom toolbar that appears only in samples (see Figure 5-5), and then tap Buy for *price*. In the figure, the price of the book is $9.73.

A second method is to purchase the book when you reach the end of the sample, as shown in Figure 5-6. Just tap the Buy Now link to purchase the book.

Sampling books on multiple devices

You can have multiple Kindles as well as other devices running the Kindle application (PCs, smartphones, and so on) registered to your Kindle account. You can register a new Kindle Paperwhite either from the device or from your computer via your Amazon account (see Chapter 2 to find out how to register your Kindle Paperwhite). For other devices, download the Kindle app and register using the device. More details on this process are in Chapter 4.

If you search or browse for Kindle content from your computer, you can send a sample to any of the devices registered to your Kindle account, including devices that run the Kindle app, such as the iPhone, an Android phone or tablet, or other PCs. If you search for content on your Kindle Paperwhite, you can send a sample only to the Kindle Paperwhite on which you're doing the searching. Samples are not saved to the Cloud; they are sent only to the specified device.

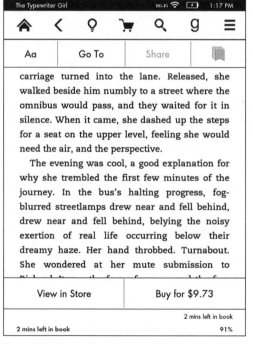

Figure 5-5: The toolbars you see in a book sample.

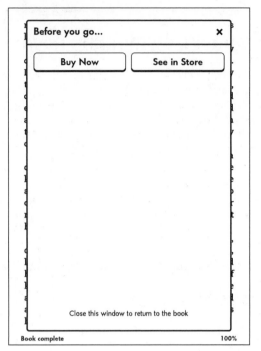

Figure 5-6: Buy the e-book when you finish the sample.

Note that for these options, you'll see a prompt to turn on wireless if necessary.

When you choose a Buy option (as opposed to visiting the store) you're taken to the book's product page at Amazon. Even though you see this page, you can't browse — the purchase is made immediately and your account is charged, as shown in Figure 5-7.

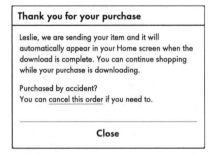

Figure 5-7: The screen you see when you purchase a book.

Note, however, that you can cancel the purchase from the screen shown in Figure 5-7. If you cancel the purchase, a screen similar to the one shown in Figure 5-8 is displayed.

Order cancelled

Leslie, you have cancelled this order.

A refund will be applied to your method of payment. If the title has already downloaded to your device, it will be removed shortly.

Close

Figure 5-8: A cancelled purchase on the Kindle Paperwhite.

After you purchase the book, your Kindle Paperwhite automatically takes you to the correct location in the book (where you left off in the sample) and deletes the sample from your device.

You can't buy e-books or other content from your Kindle Paperwhite without a wireless connection, either Wi-Fi or 3G. On the other hand, if you buy an e-book while browsing on your PC and send it to your Kindle, that purchase is queued and sent to your Kindle the next time you turn on wireless, whether it be minutes, days, or weeks later.

Locating superior subscription content

Kindle Paperwhite content isn't restricted to just e-books. In fact, one of the earliest selling points of the device was the capability to subscribe to Kindle versions of popular magazines, newspapers, and blogs. This type of content has been steadily increasing over the years. At present, several hundred magazines, newspapers, and blogs are available.

You have two options available for acquiring this type of content — an ongoing subscription or the purchase of a single issue. Per issue prices for a subscription will be less than the price to purchase a single issue, and both will _usually_ be less than a traditional subscription or a print purchase. I say _usually_ because you may find a bargain or deeply discounted subscription price that would be less than a Kindle subscription. If price is the determining factor, do your homework and shop around. On the other hand, if decreasing the clutter in your home is important and you want the convenience of wireless delivery daily, weekly, or monthly, you may find that a Kindle subscription is a viable option.

Some subscription content is available for free online, such as certain newspapers. So why pay for a Kindle Paperwhite subscription? If you commute on a train or a bus, the convenience of having the paper on your Kindle Paperwhite might be the deciding factor. On the other hand, if you like to read the paper on your computer, a subscription might not be a smart purchase. Keep in mind that Kindle subscriptions don't include advertising, whereas online periodicals often do.

Further, some online periodicals restrict content and make it available only to subscribers. For example, *The New York Times* limits nonsubscribers to ten articles per month online. Subscribers have unlimited access to the online edition, the complete archives of *The New York Times,* plus the convenience of having the paper delivered directly to the Kindle Paperwhite every morning at 4 a.m. (EST).

All Kindle subscriptions come with a minimum 14-day (newspapers) or 30-day (magazines) free trial. Special promotions may be offered with 90-day free trials for subscription content. You can cancel any time during the trial, whether it is 14, 30, or 90 days. If you don't cancel, your subscription begins automatically at the end of the trial period. Of course, you can cancel a subscription at any time, even after subscribing; you'll receive a pro-rated refund on the unused portion. Please note that the trial (14, 30, or 90 days) is a one-time option — if you cancel and then decide later you want to subscribe, even if many months have passed, your new paid subscription starts immediately.

Kindle subscriptions can be confusing because they have lots of quirks that are generally not an issue with e-books. Recognize that many of these exist because of the way the publisher has decided to format and distribute the content, and thus these issues are not under the control of Amazon. Here are some things to be aware of:

- ✔ **The Kindle Paperwhite is a grayscale device.** Magazines and newspapers that rely heavily on color photographs don't look the same on the Kindle Paperwhite. For this reason, your reading experience may not be pleasurable.

- ✔ **Content in the print edition may not be included in the Kindle subscription version.** For example, the *New Yorker* doesn't include its full complement of cartoons, and *National Geographic* doesn't include all the pictures found in the print edition. You should definitely take advantage of the free trial to determine whether you will find the content, as presented, satisfactory.

- ✔ **Not all periodicals are available for all devices, such as smartphones and the Kindle for PC app.** Which devices are supported is clearly identified on the subscription page. For example, if you hope to read your subscription to the *New Yorker* on your iPhone, you're out of luck.

✔ **Unlike e-books, subscription content can be read only on one Kindle.** You can't share subscriptions among devices, although you can change the device to which the subscription is delivered.

✔ **Only recent issues of newspapers and magazines and recent blog entries remain available on your device.** Older issues of e-newspapers and e-magazines and older blog entries are deleted automatically from your Kindle Paperwhite to make room for additional content.

Older issues of newspapers and magazines appear inside the Periodicals: Back Issues grouping, which usually appears at the end of the content listing. Select the grouping by tapping it. The screen displays the back issues you have on your Kindle Paperwhite. Older newspaper and magazine issues are automatically deleted to free space for new content. The word *Expiring* next to a magazine or newspaper issue indicates that it'll be deleted soon.

If you want to keep a copy of an issue on your Kindle Paperwhite, follow these steps:

1. **Open the specific issue from the listing of periodicals.**

2. **Tap the top of the screen to display the toolbar.**

3. **Tap Menu⇨Keep This Issue.**

When you choose to keep an issue, Keep will be displayed to the right of the title. Another way to keep an issue is to tap and hold down (long tap) on its title. When the pop-up menu appears, select Keep This Issue.

You can delete a saved issue by following the preceding steps but selecting Do Not Keep This Issue from the menu in Step 3.

Expanding on the traditional: Looking for games and apps

Games, such as Mahjong, Solitaire, and Blackjack, are also available for your Kindle Paperwhite. Some people are purists and believe that the Kindle Paperwhite should be used only for reading; others like having the option of playing a game every now and then. Given that many games are offered for free or put on sale on a regular basis, go ahead and download one and see what you think. I've become enamored with "Every Word", an anagram-type word game developed by Amazon. The touchscreen on the Kindle Paperwhite is ideal for playing this game.

In general, games are played individually, so wireless doesn't need to be on to play a game.

Games can't be sampled — if you're interested in playing Blackjack, you need to buy it. Therefore, it's a good idea to read the reviews posted at Amazon to decide whether the format and method of playing will be acceptable to you.

Not all the Kindle games that are for sale at Amazon work on the Kindle Paperwhite. Make sure that you see the name of your Kindle Paperwhite in the Deliver To drop-down list (under the Buy Now button) before making a purchase.

Kindle content, including games, can be returned within seven days for a refund. You can return e-books through Manage Your Kindle at your Amazon account. To return games, however, you must contact customer service directly; you can't process a return for a game from your Kindle Paperwhite or from your Kindle account at Amazon.

Checking Out Other Online Stores

As I mention earlier in this chapter, you don't have to purchase e-books from Amazon. E-bookstores are popping up all over the Internet, and with the popularity of the Kindle family of e-readers, most of these stores sell Kindle-compatible content. Publishers may also sell content directly from their websites. Exploring different options allows you to find some hidden gems. Similarly, if you have specific reading preferences — romance or science fiction, for example — specialized stores may have more in-depth selections and greater availability of titles in your genre of interest.

The following list is not exhaustive but is a sampling of what can be found at various online booksellers:

- ✔ **General indie (independently published) e-books:** Smashwords (www.smashwords.com)

- ✔ **Romance:** All Romance eBooks (www.allromanceebooks.com)

- ✔ **Science fiction, speculative fiction, and paranormal romance:** Baen (www.baen.com)

- ✔ **Nonfiction:** Omnilit (www.omnilit.com/)

- ✔ **Gay, lesbian, bisexual, and transgender fiction:** LGBT e-Bookshop (www.lgbtbookshop.com/)

- ✔ **Horror and dark fiction:** Darkfuse (www.darkfuse.com)

Buying from an e-bookseller

In general, purchasing from an e-bookseller is a straightforward process that involves the following steps:

1. **Register for an account with the seller.**

   The seller usually requires your name, address, and e-mail address, as well as information about your preferred form of payment (credit card or PayPal are typical).

   Some sites e-mail your Kindle purchases directly to your Kindle Paperwhite. If that's the case with the seller, enter the information it needs when you register.

   You can find your Kindle Paperwhite's e-mail address in the Manage Your Kindle section of your Amazon account. You can also find it directly from your Kindle Paperwhite. Tap Menu⇨Settings⇨Device Options⇨Personalize Your Kindle. The Send-to-Kindle Email is the fourth item in the list that appears. (See Chapter 7 for instructions on how to change your Kindle Paperwhite's e-mail address.)

2. **Add the e-bookseller to the approved list of senders who can deliver content to your Kindle Paperwhite.**

   To do this, on your computer:

   a. **Log in to your account at Amazon, choose the Manage Your Kindle option, and in the column on the left side of the page, click Personal Document Settings.**

   Your Kindle Approved e-mail list is in the middle of the page.

   b. **Add the partial e-mail address for the e-bookseller by clicking the Add a New Approved E-mail Address link.**

   Adding a partial e-mail address, such as `@ebook-seller.com`, authorizes multiple senders from that account to send content to your Kindle Paperwhite.

Make sure to add your own e-mail address(es) to your Kindle Approved e-mail list so that you can send documents to your Kindle Paperwhite.

When you e-mail content to your Kindle Paperwhite, Amazon charges 15 cents per megabyte with a 3G wireless connection but has no charge for content delivered via Wi-Fi. Note that this fee applies to users in the United States. 3G wireless transfers are 99 cents per megabyte outside the United States.

If you set your maximum delivery charge to zero cents under Whispernet Delivery Options in your Personal Document Settings, Amazon will deliver e-mailed content only when you have a Wi-Fi connection.

3. **Browse and identify e-books you want to buy and then add them to your shopping cart.**

4. **At the time of purchase, select the format for your e-book.**

   Ideally, you want to buy e-books with a PRC extension, the preferred format for the Kindle Paperwhite. If PRC isn't available, look for MOBI. Other, less desirable choices are TXT or PDF.

Do not purchase e-books that are listed as secure Mobipocket or secure MOBI because they do not work on the Kindle Paperwhite!

5. **Complete your purchase by either having the file e-mailed to your Kindle Paperwhite (if that's an option through the site) or downloading the file to your computer.**

Files purchased outside Amazon are *not* stored in the Cloud. You need to back up the files on your computer. Some e-booksellers offer a digital archive of purchases you've made. Read the terms of service to see whether they offer this feature. You may want to check for restrictions on the number of files that can be stored and the length of time that your digital library will remain active.

An e-bookseller might go out of business, so it's a good idea to back up content you purchase from sources other than Amazon.

Choosing a compatible file format for purchased e-books

The following formats are compatible with the Kindle Paperwhite:

- ✔ **AZW** is the proprietary format developed by Amazon for its Kindle-compatible e-books. Content purchased from Amazon has an AZW extension; note that AZW may be followed by a number, such as 1, 2, or 3.

- ✔ **MOBI** is a file format developed by Mobipocket; it's widely used and compatible with the Kindle Paperwhite. Note, however, that secure Mobipocket or secure MOBI files do *not* work on a Kindle Paperwhite.

✔ **PRC,** which stands for *Palm Resource Compiler,* is equivalent to MOBI and is the standard file format for books purchased at sites other than Amazon for the Kindle family of e-readers.

✔ **TXT** is a simple text file.

✔ **PDF** is the Adobe Portable Document Format. The last few generations of Kindle e-readers, including the Kindle Paperwhite, have a built-in PDF reader. You can send or e-mail the file to your Kindle Paperwhite or copy it to the Kindle Paperwhite via USB. Details on sending files are discussed in Chapter 7.

DOC and *DOCX* are files created by Microsoft Word, a word-processing program. A Word document can be converted to work on the Kindle Paperwhite. The easiest method for conversion is to send the file to your Kindle Paperwhite using the Send to Kindle app from Amazon. You can also e-mail the file to your Kindle e-mail address. I discuss these options in Chapter 7.

ePub is a common file format that you may encounter; note that ePub formatted books are *not* compatible with the Kindle Paperwhite.

Transferring files from your computer to the Kindle Paperwhite

Although e-mailing or sending a document to your Kindle Paperwhite is fast and easy (see Chapter 7), connecting your Kindle via USB cable and transferring books via drag-and-drop is a simple process too.

Both Macintosh and Windows users can download and transfer Kindle content and personal documents from their computers to their Kindles through the USB connection. When the Kindle is plugged into a computer, it appears as a removable mass-storage device.

To transfer files via USB cable, your computer must meet the following system requirements:

✔ **PC:** Windows 2000 or later

✔ **Macintosh:** Mac OS X 10.2 or later

✔ **USB port:** An available port or an attached USB hub with an available port

To connect your Kindle Paperwhite to your computer:

1. **Plug the larger end of the USB cable into an available USB port or a powered USB hub connected to your computer, and connect the other end of the USB cable to the micro-USB port on the bottom of the Kindle Paperwhite.**

   When connected to the PC, the Kindle Paperwhite goes into USB drive mode and its battery is recharged by the computer. Wireless service is temporarily shut off. The Kindle isn't usable as a reading device while in USB drive mode but returns to your reading location when you eject the device from your computer.

2. **When your Kindle Paperwhite is connected, simply drag and drop (or copy and paste) the file from your computer's hard drive to the Kindle Paperwhite's Documents folder.**

   If you put the file in the root drive instead of the Documents folder, it won't appear on the Home screen of your Kindle Paperwhite.

Discovering Sources of Free Content

You can find many sources of free content. The quickest and easiest way to find free e-books, games, and other offers that are available at Amazon is to search the Top 100 Free category in the Kindle Store. Not all the free e-books are restricted to classics; various publishers run special promotions to entice readers to try new authors — often on the eve of a new e-book release. You need to be quick, though — many times the freebie is available only for a few days before it goes back to the regular price.

Another option is to visit KBoards at www.kboards.com/. Members there maintain a monthly thread that lists free e-books from a variety of sites. The list is updated regularly to show when the e-book is no longer free.

When you order an e-book from Amazon, even if it is free, it appears as a purchase with a purchase price of $0.00. You receive a confirmation e-mail, too, so don't be surprised. Yes, you have "bought" the e-book, even if you didn't have to pay anything for it. Free books from Amazon are stored in the Cloud and available to you, even if the free promotion ends.

DRM and piracy

Digital Rights Management (DRM) is a method for securing digital content so that an e-book (or music file or whatever else) can be read or used only on an authorized device.

When Amazon first started selling Kindle e-books, they were encoded so that they were specific to the device. Authors who sold through their Desktop Publishing (DTP) platform were required to upload DRM-encrypted files. The DTP requirements have since been eased so that DRM is no longer required, although many books sold on Amazon still have DRM.

A discussion of the ethics of DRM is beyond the scope of this e-book. Just know that before you buy an e-book from a site other than Amazon, make sure that the format is compatible with your Kindle Paperwhite and isn't encoded in such a way that would render the e-book unreadable.

Piracy is the other side of the DRM coin — or what DRM is trying to prevent. If a file isn't encoded, it can be shared freely with any number of other readers. *Piracy* is stealing e-books and taking money out of the pocket of the author and publisher. Please don't engage in this illegal activity.

Read the fine print carefully. Many free offers are restricted to certain countries or territories. Make sure the price is listed as $0.00 before you opt to buy.

In addition to Amazon, a number of sites offer free e-books, all available to you legally:

- ✔ **Project Gutenberg:** One of the original free e-book sites, Project Gutenberg, at www.gutenberg.org/wiki/Main_Page, includes 42,000 books that have been digitized with the help of thousands of dedicated volunteers. All e-books were originally published by bona fide publishers; the copyrights have since expired. You can search by author or title, or browse by category, by most recently updated, or by Top 100. Project Gutenberg includes e-books in languages other than English, ranging from Afrikaans to Yiddish.

- ✔ **Internet Archive:** This site features millions of rare, out-of-print works in multiple languages and formats. It's especially useful for academic work. Visit www.archive.org/details/texts.

- ✔ **Open Library:** This site, at http://openlibrary.org, includes 20 million user-contributed items and over 1 million e-books in multiple editions and formats. Their goal is "One web page for every book ever published."

✔ **FreeTechBooks.com:** This site lists free online computer science, engineering, and programming e-books, e-textbooks, and lecture notes, which are all legally and freely available over the Internet. Go to `http://freetechbooks.com`.

✔ **manybooks.net:** You can find classic texts at `http://manybooks.net` that are copyright-free, ranging from *Alice in Wonderland* by Lewis Carroll (CreateSpace) to *Zambesi Expedition* by David Livingstone (Kessinger Publishing). You can also find new fiction by emerging authors. All the texts offered on the site are free to U.S. users. Most titles are offered in a variety of formats, including AZW, which works on the Kindle Paperwhite.

✔ **Feedbooks:** This site is another source of free, public domain e-books. Visit `www.feedbooks.com/publicdomain`.

The Feedbooks website includes a section with paid content. These e-books are *not* compatible with the Kindle Paperwhite, so don't purchase one in error! Only the free public domain e-books at Feedbooks work on your Kindle Paperwhite.

Chapter 6

Loaning, Borrowing, and Gifting

In This Chapter

▶ Letting friends borrow an e-book

▶ Borrowing books from the library

▶ Checking out the Kindle Owners' Lending Library

▶ Giving a book as a gift

*Y*our Kindle Paperwhite has several innovative features that give you new ways to lend e-books to others, borrow from libraries and Amazon (through the Kindle Owners' Lending Library), and give e-books as gifts.

Loaning Books

You can loan an e-book to anyone — even if the person doesn't have a Kindle! All you need is the person's e-mail address and a book that has loaning enabled.

You can loan e-books from your computer. Follow these steps to lend an e-book to a friend:

1. **Open a web browser on your personal computer and go to the Manage Your Kindle page (www.amazon.com/myk).**

2. **If necessary, log in.**

3. **Scroll down to view the e-books in your Kindle Library.**

4. **Hover the cursor over the Actions button for the e-book you'd like to loan, and click the Loan This Title option (if it appears).**

   You'll see this option if loaning has been enabled for the e-book.

5. Enter the person's e-mail address and name. You may also type a message if you want.

The borrower of the e-book receives an e-mail from Amazon, similar to the message shown in Figure 6-1. The borrower has seven days to accept the loan by clicking the Get Your Loaned Book Now button provided in the e-mail.

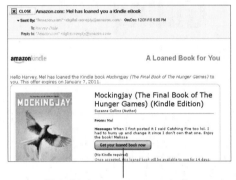

Click this button to accept the loan

Figure 6-1: When you loan an e-book, Amazon sends an e-mail to the borrower.

What if the person you've loaned the e-book to doesn't have a Kindle? No problem! You can use many devices to read Kindle e-books, as you discover in Chapter 4.

The borrower can return the loaned e-book before the 14-day loan is over. If you're reading a borrowed book and want to return it, go to the Your Kindle Library section of the Manage Your Kindle page on Amazon. Click the plus symbol (+) next to the loaned title and then click the Delete This Title link.

While an e-book from your Kindle is on loan, you can't read it. Also, you can loan a book only one time. A letter will be sent to your personal documents to remind you that the book is on loan and the annotation *On Loan* will appear next to the book in Your Kindle Library.

Currently, only e-book customers residing in the United States can loan Kindle e-books. Loans can be made to people living outside the United States, but the borrower may not be able to accept the loan, depending on geographic differences in publishing rights.

You can join Kindle community forums to participate in exchanges in which Kindle owners lend and borrow e-books. A popular forum is the Lend and Borrow Exchange link at www.kboards.com.

Lending versus sharing

When you purchase Kindle e-books from Amazon, they're associated with your Amazon account. If you have more than one Kindle device or app registered to your account, content can be shared among the devices, but it can't be shared with a device or an app registered to another account. Sharing refers specifically to sharing books among devices registered to a single Amazon account.

Although you might not mind having multiple devices on your account, keep in mind that those other devices — and their users — have access to your account to buy content using the credit card associated with the account. Even though devices on the same account can be shared, publishers may limit how many times you can download a copy simultaneously to different devices or apps. Books do not have unlimited sharing privileges.

Some Kindle e-books can be loaned to devices not registered to your account. In general, e-books that can be loaned to another Kindle owner on a different account can be lent only once, for a period of two weeks. While the e-book is on loan, it isn't available to you.

Current subscription content, such as an e-magazine or an e-newspaper, is limited to one Kindle at a time. For example, two people can't share a daily subscription to the *New York Times* and read the current day's paper at the same time on two different devices. Past issues can be downloaded to compatible devices on the same account. Subscription content cannot be loaned across accounts.

If you give a used Kindle as a gift, the content you purchased can't be given as a gift. The device must be deregistered and the previous content erased. You can deregister a Kindle Paperwhite on the device itself (in the Settings section) or from the Manage Your Devices section of your Amazon account. Follow the same steps as you did to register your Kindle Paperwhite in Chapter 2. (The options will change to deregister instead.) You can delete content by tapping Menu⇨Settings⇨Menu⇨Reset Device.

Read the License Agreement and Terms of Use at the Kindle Store. This document governs the use of e-books and digital content you download from Amazon. It can be found at www.amazon.com/kindlelicense.

Want to know whether a book can be loaned before you purchase it? From a personal computer, view the book's product page on Amazon. Scroll down to the Product Details section and look for Lending: Enabled.

Borrowing Books from the Library

Many public libraries allow Kindle e-books to be checked out. How does this work? The e-book is made available to you for a fixed amount of time — the loan period varies by library. When the loan expires, the e-book is no longer available to you, unless you check it out again or purchase it from Amazon's Kindle Store.

You can make highlights, add notes, and include bookmarks in a borrowed library e-book. Those annotations are preserved even after the e-book loan expires, in case you later decide to purchase the e-book or borrow it again.

To borrow an e-book, go to your local public library's website. If your library supports OverDrive digital e-book services, you can check out Kindle-compatible e-books. Note that you must use your library card and have online borrowing privileges. And, just as with paper books, all available copies of an e-book may be checked out. Most libraries will allow you to reserve an e-book or put it on hold.

Public library e-books for Kindle e-readers are presently available only in the United States.

 From your library's website, you can have the e-book delivered wirelessly to your Kindle or Kindle app through Wi-Fi. (They aren't distributed over a 3G connection.) Note that some publishers allow books to be transferred to your Kindle Paperwhite only by using the USB cable. These books also cannot be read on other devices such as an iPhone or a PC (using the Kindle app).

Borrowing Books from the Kindle Owners' Lending Library

If you're an Amazon Prime member, you have access to the Kindle Owners' Lending Library. Amazon Prime is a $79-a-year subscription program that provides a number of benefits to subscribers, including free shipping on Prime-eligible products; access to the Prime video library; and for Kindle owners, the opportunity to borrow books from the Kindle Owners' Lending Library.

At the time of this writing, close to 440,000 books were available, covering topics from fiction, to humor, to travel. For an overview, use your device to go to the Kindle Store and open the drop-down menu for All Categories. The Kindle Owners' Lending Library is the last item on the list.

After you select Kindle Owners' Lending Library, a screen appears listing all the books available in various categories, such as Nonfiction, Travel, and History. Tap on a topic of interest to see specific books, and then select a book that appeals to you. Figure 6-2 shows a book available for loan from the Kindle Owners' Lending Library.

Figure 6-2: You can borrow books for free.

Read the book's description and reviews. If you find a book that intrigues you, simply tap the Borrow for Free icon to download the book immediately to your Kindle Paperwhite. When you borrow a book, you'll see a screen similar to the one shown in Figure 6-3.

You can borrow one book per month. You can't borrow a new book until you return the previously borrowed book. If you aren't eligible to borrow a book (that is, you've reached your monthly quota), the option to Borrow for Free appears dimmed at the Kindle Store.

If you have a borrowed book on your Kindle Paperwhite, you'll be asked to return the book before you can borrow another, as shown in Figure 6-4. Although you can borrow only one book per month, you can keep a book on your device for as long as you want — but you won't be able to borrow a second book until you return the first one.

Thank you for borrowing this title

Leslie, we are sending your book and it will automatically appear in your Home screen when the download is complete.

Kindle Owners' Lending Library Status

You have 1 book checked out:

War Brides
by Helen Bryan
Checked out: October 18, 2013

You will be able to borrow again starting November 1, 2013.

Close

Figure 6-3: Borrowing a book from the Kindle Owners' Lending Library.

Please return your current book   ✕

You may only borrow one book at a time.

Kindle Owners' Lending Library Status

You have 1 book checked out:

Man in the Crescent Moon (Pirates of the Narrow Seas)
by M. Kei
Checked out: August 5, 2013

When you return a book, it will be removed from your Kindle. Your notes and furthest page read will be saved.

Return book

Close - I'll keep the book I have.

Figure 6-4: You must return a borrowed book before borrowing another.

Although you can use your computer to browse the Kindle Store and see books that are available for borrowing, you have to use your Kindle Paperwhite to borrow a book. You can't send a borrowed book to your Kindle Paperwhite from your computer.

If you maintain a Wish List at Amazon, you can access it from your Kindle Paperwhite and see which books on your list are available for free borrowing. Tap Settings, and then swipe the list to see additional options. Your Wish List will be at the top of the list. Tap it, and then Tap Kindle Wish List. Books that are available in the Kindle Owners' Lending Library will appear with the Prime logo.

You can also rent Kindle textbooks, which is a great option for students. See Chapter 9 for details.

Gifting Books

You can give anyone an e-book from the book's product page on Amazon. A Give as a Gift button is available for most e-books in the Kindle Store.

You can e-mail the gift directly to someone or specify when the e-mail should be sent. Recipients receive a link in the e-mail that enables them to access the e-book.

Alternatively, you can have the e-mail sent to you. Perhaps you'd like to forward the e-mail later to the giftee or you want to print the e-mail and present the gift that way.

If the recipient already owns the book you have selected, he or she can use the gift certificate toward the purchase of a different book.

 Many online e-booksellers also let you give an e-book as a gift. Details on how to do so are available at the seller's website. I list some popular e-booksellers in Chapter 5.

Chapter 7

Adding Documents

In This Chapter

▶ Understanding Kindle-friendly file formats

▶ Transferring documents from your computer

▶ Sending files from a desktop, a browser, or an Android device

▶ Sending documents by e-mail

▶ Viewing PDFs on your Kindle Paperwhite

▶ Paying fees to transfer documents

*A*fter you've had your Kindle Paperwhite for a while, you're sure to have downloaded e-books from the Kindle Store or from other online sources. But what if you want to read some of your own content on your Kindle Paperwhite? Most people have a massive collection of materials from work or school on their computers: reference manuals, lists, maps, correspondence, creative writing, and other personal documents. Wouldn't it be nice to have some of that content available on your Kindle Paperwhite as you travel or go about your daily life?

Or what if you're surfing the web and you see an interesting article or blog post and think to yourself, "I'd like to put that on my Kindle Paperwhite to read later." Guess what? You can! Amazon and the Kindle Paperwhite have some new tools to allow you to do this quickly and easily.

In this chapter, you explore how to put your own documents onto your Kindle Paperwhite. You also find out how to create documents that you might acquire from other sources. Then you discover some handy services and tools to send compatible files to your Kindle Paperwhite and to convert documents so that they're readable on your device.

Transferring Kindle-Friendly File Formats

Your Kindle Paperwhite can't read every file that's on your computer. A file has to be in a Kindle-compatible format so that the device can display it. The following list describes the Kindle-friendly file types:

- **AZW** is the Kindle format, so most files you download from the Kindle Store will have an AZW extension. Note that some files might have a number, such as 1, 2, or 3, after the AZW.

- **MOBI,** a file format developed by Mobipocket, is widely used and compatible with the Kindle Paperwhite. Note, however, that secure Mobipocket or secure MOBI files do *not* work on a Kindle Paperwhite.

- **PRC** is equivalent to MOBI and is the standard file format for the Kindle family of e-readers for content that comes from sources other than Amazon.com.

- **TXT** is a simple text file, such as one you might create with Notepad.

- **PDF:** Your Kindle Paperwhite can display files in Adobe's Portable Document Format (PDF).

Files in these formats are generally readable *natively* — that is, without needing to be converted — by your Kindle Paperwhite. So all you have to do is transfer the files onto your Kindle Paperwhite, as I describe in the next section.

If you use Windows Explorer or Finder on a Mac, you may see files with the POBI extension on your Kindle Paperwhite. Curious about these? Do you have any periodicals (newspapers or magazines) on your device? If so, they'll have the POBI extension. POBI is a variation of MOBI and enables the display of articles and sections in periodical content. To learn more about navigating in a periodical, see Chapter 4.

Copying Files from Your Computer

If your file is in one of the Kindle-compatible formats listed in the preceding section, you can transfer it directly from your computer to your Kindle Paperwhite via USB.

To transfer the files, follow these steps:

1. **Connect your Kindle Paperwhite to your computer using the USB cable.**

   Your computer recognizes your Kindle Paperwhite when it's plugged in and displays the Kindle Paperwhite as a removable drive, as shown in Figure 7-1. If you go to My Computer (PC) or Finder (Mac), your Kindle Paperwhite appears as a drive.

Your Kindle Paperwhite

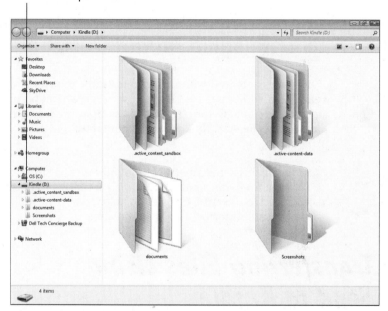

Figure 7-1: Your Kindle Paperwhite appears as a removable hard drive when connected to your computer.

2. **Double-click the drive to open it and view the folders on your Kindle Paperwhite.**

3. **Open another window and navigate to the file(s) you want to transfer to your Kindle Paperwhite.**

4. **Drag the file(s) to the Documents folder on your Kindle Paperwhite.**

   You can also use the Copy and Paste commands to move documents to the Documents folder.

5. **Eject your Kindle Paperwhite from your computer:**

- **On a Windows 8 PC:** Right-click the Kindle drive icon and choose Eject. A notification that it is safe to remove the device from the computer appears.

- **On a Windows Vista or Windows 7 PC:** Choose Start⇨Computer, and then right-click the Kindle drive icon and choose Eject. You can also left- or right-click the Safely Remove Hardware and Eject Media icon in the lower-right corner of the taskbar.

- **On a Mac:** Control-click the Kindle device icon and choose Eject.

The files you transferred are displayed on your Home screen and are available for you to view on your Kindle Paperwhite.

If files are protected with DRM, your Kindle Paperwhite cannot read them and you'll see an error message when you try to open the e-book. Before buying books from sources other than Amazon, make sure that the file is compatible with your Kindle Paperwhite.

Sideloading describes the transfer of files directly from one device to another. *Uploading* and *downloading* are terms that are commonly used to describe transferring files to or from an Internet server. What I describe here is sideloading.

Transferring Files Using Send to Kindle

If you have a document in a format that is not native to the Kindle Paperwhite (as described in the preceding section), you can send it to your device using the Send to Kindle application. The document will be converted to a compatible format and displayed on the Home screen of your Kindle Paperwhite.

To begin, go to the Send to Kindle home page at www.amazon.com/gp/sendtokindle. You'll see options for sending documents to your Kindle Paperwhite from your desktop, browser, Android device, and e-mail.

Sending from the desktop

In the From Your Desktop section of the Send to Kindle home page, click the appropriate link for your computer: PC or Mac. You see instructions on how the Send to Kindle program works and the system requirements for your computer.

Agree to the terms of service, and click Download Now to begin the download and installation process. Figure 7-2 shows the screen that appears when the program has been successfully installed.

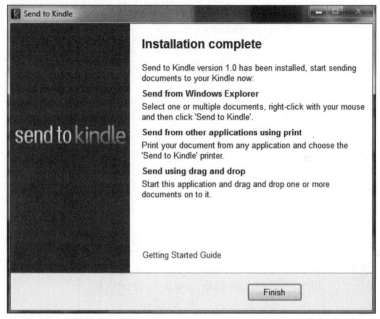

Figure 7-2: Successful installation of Send to Kindle for PC.

After the program is installed, you can access it in a variety of ways. Here are a few examples:

1. **Do one of the following:**

   - **Word processing, spreadsheets, and other productivity applications:** Choose Print.

   - **Windows Explorer (PC):** Right-click to select a document. To select multiple documents, use Control-Click or Shift-Click.

   - **Finder (Mac):** Control-click to select one or more documents.

2. **Choose Send to Kindle as your printer, and then choose Print.**

3. In the dialog box that appears:

a. **Insert a title and an author.**

b. **Choose the devices to which you want to send the document.**

You can also choose to have the document archived in your Kindle Library, which means you'll be able to download it from the Cloud later to any of your Kindles.

c. **Decide whether to use Wi-Fi delivery, which is free, or Whispernet, which may incur a charge.**

See the last section, "Paying Fees for Transferring Documents," for details.

4. Choose Send.

The document will be converted to PDF format and delivered to your Kindle Paperwhite.

Wireless must be turned on for your Kindle Paperwhite to receive documents.

If you do not see Send to Kindle on the pop-up menu that appears, you are probably trying to send a file in a format that is not compatible with your Kindle Paperwhite and cannot be converted to a PDF through the Send to Kindle process.

Sending from a browser

If you use Google Chrome or Mozilla Firefox as your browser, you can download a nifty little app that lets you send news articles, blog posts, or any other content that grabs your eye to your Kindle Paperwhite. On the Send to Kindle page, click the link for either Google Chrome or Mozilla Firefox in the From Your Browser area.

Follow the instructions for downloading the app. When the app is installed, you see a small *K* at the top right of the screen. When you click the K button in the browser, the dialog box shown in Figure 7-3 appears.

You can send directly to your Kindle Paperwhite, preview before sending, or send selected text. After you make your choice, the content will be formatted and will appear on the Home screen of your Kindle Paperwhite in a few minutes — as long as wireless is turned on.

Figure 7-3: Send to Kindle in Google Chrome.

Sending from an Android device

If you have an Android device, you can send documents to your Kindle Paperwhite using the Send to Kindle for Android app. On the Send to Kindle page, click the link in the From Your Android device area to download the application and follow the instructions.

Then you can use the Share feature found in many apps to send documents to your Kindle Paperwhite. Supported file types include Microsoft Word (DOC, DOCX); PDF; images (JPG, JPEG, GIF, PNG, BMP); and Kindle format (MOBI, AZW).

Sending from E-Mail

The Send to Kindle application certainly makes converting and transferring documents quick and easy. However, e-mail is a reliable standby to use for file transfer.

You can use e-mail also when you don't want to sideload content onto your Kindle Paperwhite with the USB cable.

File types that can be transferred through e-mail

You can send the following types of files to your Kindle Paperwhite using the unique e-mail address for your device. Note that these files must be *unprotected* (that is, not protected by DRM) to be readable on your Kindle Paperwhite:

- ✔ Microsoft Word (DOC or DOCX)
- ✔ PDF (PDF)
- ✔ HyperText Markup Language (HTML, HTM)
- ✔ Plain text (TXT)
- ✔ Rich text (RTF)
- ✔ Kindle format (MOBI, AZW)
- ✔ Graphics (JPG, GIF, PNG, or BMP)

Utilizing the Kindle Paperwhite e-mail address

To convert your personal documents so you can read them on your Kindle Paperwhite, send them to the e-mail address associated with your Kindle Paperwhite: *yourname*@kindle.com, where *yourname* is the unique name identified with your Kindle Paperwhite. This e-mail address was created automatically when you registered your Kindle Paperwhite. You can change the e-mail address, if you want; the steps to do so are described shortly.

Discovering your Paperwhite's e-mail address

To find out what your Kindle Paperwhite's e-mail address is, follow these steps:

1. **Tap Menu⇨Settings.**
2. **Tap Device Options⇨Personalize Your Kindle.**

   The Personalize Your Kindle screen appears. Send-to-Kindle E-Mail, the fourth item in the list, displays the e-mail associated with your Kindle Paperwhite.

Changing your Paperwhite's e-mail address

To change your Kindle Paperwhite's e-mail address, you must do so from your Amazon account on your computer. Follow these steps:

1. Go to www.amazon.com/myk.

2. **If prompted, enter your e-mail address and password.**

3. **Click the Sign In Using Our Secure Server button.**

4. **From the left menu, under Your Kindle Account, choose Personal Document Settings.**

   Your Kindle Paperwhite and its associated e-mail address appear.

5. **Click Edit and input a new address.**

   If you create an e-mail address that is already in use, you'll be prompted to modify it or create another.

6. **Click the Update button to save.**

To send an e-mail to your Kindle Paperwhite, you need to approve your own e-mail address and any others that might send content to your device. This can be accomplished only through your Amazon account, not from the Kindle Paperwhite.

Approving an e-mail address

Amazon adds a level of security to the e-mail transfer process by limiting which e-mail addresses can be used to send documents to your @kindle.com e-mail address. This prevents unauthorized users from sending documents to your Kindle Paperwhite and potentially running up document transfer charges.

You manage this approved e-mail list from the Manage Your Kindle page. To approve an e-mail address so it can send content to your Kindle Paperwhite, follow these steps:

1. Go to www.amazon.com/myk.

2. **If prompted, enter your e-mail address and password.**

3. **Click the Sign In Using Our Secure Server button.**

4. **From the left menu, under Your Kindle Account, choose Personal Document Settings.**

   The list of approved e-mail addresses is in the center of the screen under the heading, Approved Personal Document E-Mail List. If you have not previously approved any e-mail addresses, the list will be blank.

5. **Click Add a New Approved E-Mail Address.**

6. **Enter the e-mail address you want to approve, and then click Add Address.**

7. **To add and approve additional e-mail addresses, repeat Step 6.**

   The approved addresses are listed in the table in the center of the screen, with the option to delete them on the right (if you later choose to do so).

Make sure to include your own e-mail address (or addresses, if you have multiple e-mail accounts from which you might be sending documents to your Kindle Paperwhite) so that you can send documents to your device.

 Many e-book retailers allow you to set up your account so that purchases you make are e-mailed automatically to your Kindle Paperwhite. In essence, this mimics the wireless delivery service that Amazon offers. If you want to take advantage of this, make sure to add the e-mail address of the e-bookseller to your approved list of e-mail addresses.

 If you want to allow documents to be sent from anyone from a particular domain, don't include a username. For example, adding `@mycompany.com` authorizes anyone with an e-mail address matching that domain name to send documents to your Kindle Paperwhite. However, you are responsible for any charges for documents sent from those e-mail addresses via Whispernet to your Kindle Paperwhite. Transferring files via Wi-Fi is free. If you set the maximum charge for Whispernet Delivery over 3G to $0, personal documents will be sent only via Wi-Fi even if you have 3G. You can make this change in the Personal Documents Settings.

More options for converting documents

If you want to read a file on your Kindle Paperwhite that's in an unsupported file type, you can install software on your computer that can read different file types and then convert those files to Kindle-compatible formats. One such option is calibre (`www.calibre-ebook.com`), which is available for PC or Mac. The calibre program can convert e-books in a host of formats — including CBZ, CBR, CBC, CHM, EPUB, FB2, HTML, LIT, LRF, MOBI, ODT, PDF, PRC, PDB, PML, RB, RTF, SNB, TCR, and TXT — to various other formats, including the Kindle-compatible MOBI format.

Sending the files

When you know your Kindle Paperwhite's e-mail address and you've added your personal e-mail address to the Approved Personal Document E-Mail List (see the preceding section), transferring files is simple:

1. **Open your e-mail program or your e-mail web page. Log on to your account, if necessary.**

2. **Create a new message. In the To text box, enter the e-mail address of your Kindle Paperwhite.**

3. **Attach the document you want to transfer to your Kindle Paperwhite.**

   There's no need to specify a subject or to provide text in the body of the message. Amazon recommends that each personal document be no larger than 50MB.

4. **Click Send.**

   If you're connected in a Wi-Fi area (or with 3G for Kindle Paperwhites so enabled), you receive the converted file on your Kindle Paperwhite in about five minutes. Very large files can take longer to convert and receive.

When you send personal documents to your Kindle Paperwhite, they're stored automatically in your Kindle Library at Amazon. You can store up to 5 gigabytes of personal documents in the archive.

If you're sending a PDF file and would like to take advantage of features on the Kindle Paperwhite, such as changing font size and making notes, convert the file to Kindle format (AZW) by typing **CONVERT** in the subject line of your message.

Reading PDF Documents

Some of the personal documents that you load on your Kindle Paperwhite may be PDF documents. The Kindle Paperwhite can read PDF documents *natively* — in other words, without converting them.

The Kindle Paperwhite handles PDF documents differently from how it handles text in the usual Kindle format:

- PDF documents are displayed with the text and graphics laid out exactly as in the original PDF document. You can't change the layout, font size, typeface, line spacing, and words per line.

✔ You can zoom in on a PDF document by unpinching (placing two fingers on the screen and moving your fingers apart). Note that this is different than increasing the font size. The text doesn't reflow; instead, you see an enlarged view of a section of the screen. You can then pan around the screen by sliding your finger on the display. To zoom out, pinch the screen (move two fingers together). You can't turn the page while zooming in.

You can adjust the contrast of the displayed document by tapping the Menu icon.

✔ At the bottom of the screen, your Kindle Paperwhite displays the original PDF document's page numbers.

Why would you want to read a document in PDF format? Many PDF documents are highly formatted with columns, tables, and figures that do not convert well to Kindle Paperwhite format. Although you lose the ability to make notes and marks in a PDF, you are able to read the document as originally presented.

The Kindle Paperwhite does not support reading PDFs in Landscape mode.

Do you want to use Kindle Paperwhite features such as changing font size and making notes? When e-mailing the PDF file, simply convert the file to Kindle format (AZW) by typing **CONVERT** in the subject line of your message. If you do this, look carefully at the formatting of the PDF to make sure that a converted file is going to be acceptable to you for reading.

Paying Fees for Transferring Documents

If you have a Wi-Fi–only Kindle Paperwhite, all your documents will be delivered by Wi-Fi without charge. If you're in an area where Wi-Fi is not available, your documents will be queued and delivered when Wi-Fi is available.

If you have a 3G device and Wi-FI is not available, the document can be delivered using Whispernet — that is, over a 3G network. Amazon does not charge a monthly fee for 3G, but you do incur a charge for receiving documents this way. At present, the fee is $.15 per megabyte for customers in the United States and $.99 per megabyte when traveling outside the United States and for Kindle users living outside the United States.

Wireless file transfer isn't available in all countries. For the latest availability information, go to www.amazon.com/myk, log in if necessary, and click the Kindle Support link. Scroll down to the Wireless Delivery section. Even if wireless file transfer isn't available, you can still use the Kindle e-mail conversion service and then transfer the converted files to your Kindle Paperwhite via USB.

You can set a limit on the charges allowed for personal documents to be transferred. Go to the Manage Your Kindle page (www.amazon.com/myk), and click the Personal Document Settings link in the left column. Scroll down to the middle of the page to the section headed Whispernet Delivery Option. Choose Edit (on the right) to change the maximum amount that you will be charged (from $0 to $49.50 with a default of $2.50). If you try to convert a document that exceeds that charge, it won't be delivered and you'll be notified by e-mail. Some Kindle Paperwhite users set the limit at $0 to ensure that all personal documents are transferred via Wi-Fi and thus incur no charges.

Chapter 8

Expanding the Reading Experience

In This Chapter

▶ Digging deeper with the dictionary, Vocabulary Builder, translations, and X-ray

▶ Sharing books and recommendations on Goodreads, Facebook, Twitter

▶ Listening and reading with Whispersync for Voice

▶ Browsing the web with your Kindle Paperwhite

Although the Kindle Paperwhite is first and foremost a *reading device,* it does offer several features that go beyond reading. You can look up words with the dictionary and memorize their definitions with Vocabulary Builder, make notes, highlight text, translate words from English to other languages and vice versa, dig deeper with the X-ray feature, browse the web, and post comments and interesting quotes on Goodreads, Facebook, and Twitter.

In this chapter, I look at these features — and go beyond reading with your Kindle Paperwhite!

Easy Dictionary Look-Up

One of the most useful Kindle Paperwhite features is the built-in dictionary. The dictionary is easy to access and makes it swift and painless to find the definition of an unknown word.

To display a dictionary definition of a word, long-tap (that is, tap and hold down on) a word. The selected word is highlighted as white text on a black background. When you release your finger, a dictionary definition for the word appears onscreen in a pop-up box, as shown in Figure 8-1. To clear the definition, tap anywhere outside the pop-up box.

Figure 8-1: Displaying the definition of the word *counterfeiter*.

In the definition box, note two additional tabs: X-Ray and Wikipedia. Tap X-Ray to display additional information about the selected word. Likewise, if your device is not in Airplane mode, you can tap Wikipedia to open a Wikipedia page with information about your selected word. Note that the information provided by the three resources may be similar. I dig a little deeper into the X-ray feature later in the chapter.

X-Ray is not active in all books nor is it active for all words. When this is the case, the option will appear dimmed.

At the bottom of the definition box are two additional choices: Search and More. Tap Search to display the menu shown in Figure 8-2. You have three choices: This Book searches for the word in the current book, All Text searches for the word on your Kindle Paperwhite, and Kindle Store finds all titles that have the word — it doesn't search for every instance of the word in the Kindle Store! Results of the search for *Bombay* returned 315 hits for the book; 3 hits on my Kindle (which includes the present book with 315 instances of the word); and 176 titles in the Kindle Store.

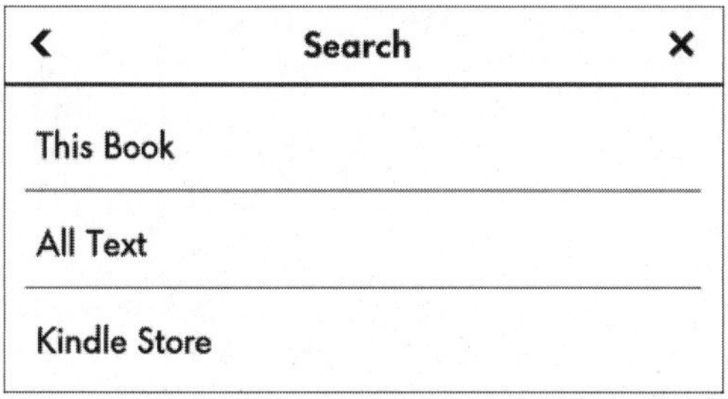

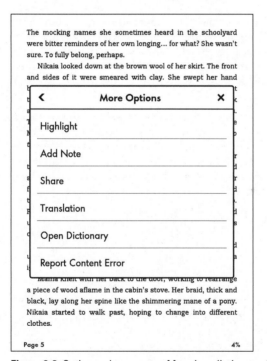

Figure 8-2: The menu you see when you tap Search from the definition of a word.

The definition box also includes a More button. Tap that button to display the screen as shown in Figure 8-3.

Figure 8-3: Options when you tap More in a dictionary definition.

You have the following options:

✔ **Highlight:** Highlight the word on the screen. Note that once the word is highlighted, the choice on the More Options menu changes to Delete. This option deletes the highlighting, not the word.

✔ **Add Note:** Add a note regarding the word. When you return to the book, word is highlighted with a superscripted number. Tap the number to read your note. To close the note, tap the X in the upper-right corner.

✔ **Share:** Share the word (and any commentary) on Goodreads and, if you want, Facebook and Twitter. Let your friends know how smart you are! (Social sharing is discussed in more detail in an upcoming section.)

✔ **Translation:** Translate the word from English to one of 16 other languages, including Chinese, Hindi, and Norwegian. You can also translate from other languages to English. The Kindle Paperwhite will even determine the source language for you. Figure 8-4 shows the translation of the word *paix* from French to English.

✔ **Open Dictionary:** Open the default dictionary at the definition of the word. In this way, you can read a more detailed definition or navigate quickly to linked entries. To return to your book, tap the Back icon. You may need to tap it several times, depending on how much exploring you did in the dictionary.

✔ **Report Content Error:** Report errors, such as typos, formatting, or other problems, directly to Amazon. Is a word misspelled or is incorrect punctuation used? Here's your chance to report it. Amazon has made a concerted effort to have publishers correct errors in their Kindle editions so that readers receive the highest quality books available.

The Kindle Paperwhite has two dictionaries: the default *New Oxford American Dictionary* and *Oxford Dictionary of English* (both from Oxford University Press). You can change the default dictionary as follows:

1. **Tap Menu⇨Settings.**

2. **Tap Device Options⇨Language and Dictionaries⇨Dictionaries.**

   The active dictionary appears.

3. **Tap the active dictionary to change to a different dictionary.**

   A list of available dictionaries stored on the device appears.

4. Change the default dictionary by tapping the radio button on the right.

The radio button that is darkened (filled in) indicates which dictionary is selected as the default.

Worth, the founding father of *haute couture*, and Albert Edward, Prince of Wales.

Worth, an expatriate English dressmaker who had set up shop in Paris' rue de la Paix, was

Translation ✕

From: French ▾   To: English ▾

Peace,

About Translation

different bodices or tailoring, this or that amount of lace, a lighter velvet or a heavier brocade. They would never humiliate a reception gown, for instance, by wearing it to the theater. And they didn't waste the designer's time. When Charles Worth deigned to dress a woman, she must mind him to the last piece of lace. He didn't want to pour out his genius on

9 hrs 30 mins left in book   11%

Figure 8-4: Translation of a word from French to English.

Stored in your Kindle Library at your Amazon account are several foreign language dictionaries, including Spanish, French, and Portuguese. Go to www.amazon.com/myk to access your library. Any (or all) of these dictionaries can be delivered to your Kindle Paperwhite. If you change the language on your device, the corresponding language dictionary becomes the default. Note that you won't see the dictionaries if you look in the Cloud on your Kindle Paperwhite; you have to go to your Kindle Library using your computer.

Vocabulary Builder

By default, every word you look up in the dictionary is added to a list that you can access using Vocabulary Builder. From any book, tap Menu — Vocabulary Builder. The screen shown in

Figure 8-5 appears, listing the words you've looked up. Tap a word to see its definition. On the menu that appears, you can tap the Usage tab to see how the word was used in the book.

Vocabulary Builder		Wi-Fi 📶 🔋 3:45 PM
🏠 ‹ 💡 🛒 g ☰		
Words | Books		Learning (35) ▼
chimney	fire	restaurants
intimacy	Ghani	Bombay
visitor	relationship	counterfeiter
humility	The	India
Coronado	people	grieved
Bruiser	examination	renovations
anywhere	COMPARABLE	ontologically
and	incomparable	sentient
Thanks	camel	language
festival	Assamese	to
Flashcards		

Figure 8-5: Word list in Vocabulary Builder.

To change the view from a list of words to the list of books in which you've searched for words, tap Books at the top of the screen. The screen shown in Figure 8-6 appears. Tap the arrow to the right of a book's title to see all the words you researched in that book. You can then tap a word to see its definition and its usage in the book.

Your Kindle Paperwhite includes a Flashcards feature to help you learn the words on your vocabulary list. At the bottom of Figure 8-6, tap Flashcards to display a screen like the one shown in Figure 8-7. Use the arrows or swipe to page forward and backward through the list. Each flashcard shows the word in context in the book you were reading — if you can't remember the definition, tap See Definition to refresh your memory. When you've learned the word, tap Mark as Mastered to remove it from the active list. Tap Exit Flashcards in the upper left to return to the active word list.

Figure 8-6: Book view in Vocabulary Builder.

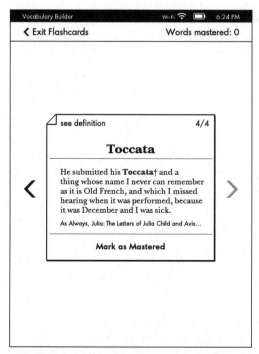

Figure 8-7: Use flashcards to reinforce definitions.

You can also mark a word as Mastered from the Dictionary definition screen.

Vocabulary Builder appears on your Home screen in your list of books. Tap Vocabulary Builder to open it, just as you would a book. You can access Vocabulary Builder (after you've activated it the first time) also from the menu. If your list on the Home screen is sorted by Recent and Vocabulary Builder is the most recent item you've viewed, it will be at the top of the list. If your Home screen is sorted by Collections, Vocabulary Builder will be the first item in the list after the listing of collections.

 Kindle Free Time, which is discussed in Chapter 9, works the same way after it has been activated, as does the My Clippings folder.

As noted, Vocabulary Builder is turned on by default. To turn it off, tap Menu⇨Settings⇨Reading Options. Switch the toggle to Off. Now Vocabulary Builder will not appear on your Home screen and the menu option for Vocabulary Builder will appear dimmed. Any words you look up in the dictionary will not be added to your vocabulary list, but any words you've looked up previously will be retained.

Utilizing Highlights and Notes

As you're reading, you may want to highlight text to refer to later or to add your own notes to a particular passage. You may even want to make a Facebook post or Twitter tweet that includes an excerpt from the e-book. The touchscreen makes it particularly convenient for you to make these marks, or *annotations:*

- ✔ **Highlights** shade a section of text to draw attention to it.
- ✔ **Notes** are text you type, much like when you jot notes in the margins of a printed book.

These annotations are stored on your Kindle Paperwhite and are backed up at Amazon — as long as the annotations backup feature is turned on. To check whether this is the case, tap Menu⇨Settings⇨Reading Options⇨Notes & Highlights. Make sure the toggle switch next to Annotations Backup is set to On. This setting enables you to recover your notes if you lose your Kindle Paperwhite or upgrade to another model. If you borrow a book from the Kindle Owners' Lending Library or rent a textbook, your annotations are preserved, even when you return the book. See Chapter 6 to find out more about the library and Chapter 9 for information on renting texts.

To make an annotation, select text in your book by touching your finger to a word and dragging your finger across the screen. As you do so, the selected text turns white on a black background.

When you release your finger, a pop-up window provides these options: Add Note, Highlight, Share, and More. In the following sections, I look at each option.

Annotating is disabled in book samples. You can't add notes, highlights, or bookmarks or share excerpts when viewing a book sample.

Highlighting text

With the desired text selected (see the preceding section), tap the Highlight button. The text is highlighted in the book — appearing as black text on a gray background.

To delete a highlight, select any of the highlighted words by touching and dragging across them or by long-tapping. A Delete button appears in a pop-up window; tap Delete to remove the highlight.

What if the text you want to highlight spans more than one page? Just tap at the beginning and keep dragging to the next page. The text will continue to be highlighted. If you want to see everything on one page, adjust the font size to get all your desired text on the screen. Or you can adjust the starting point of the displayed text by changing the location. Touch the top of the screen to display the toolbar, and then tap Menu⇨Go To⇨Page or Location. Enter a location slightly different than the current location to shift the starting point of the displayed text, until all your desired text is displayed.

An interesting thing about highlights is that you can view highlights that *other readers* have made. Amazon collects this information and highlights passages in your book that have been highlighted frequently by other readers. Your Kindle Paperwhite displays how many people have highlighted that particular passage.

Although this can be intriguing, some readers find the display of popular highlights distracting. To turn off these popular highlights, follow these steps:

1. **Tap Menu⇨Settings⇨Reading Options⇨Notes & Highlights.**

    Popular Highlights is one of the Reading Options listed.

2. **Tap the On/Off toggle to deactivate the Popular Highlights option.**

If you don't want to share your highlighted passages with Amazon, turn off the Annotations Backup option in the Reading Options page under Settings. If you do this, your annotations aren't backed up by Amazon, and they won't appear on other devices registered to your Amazon account.

Taking notes

Want to make margin notes in your books? You can with your Kindle Paperwhite. Adding notes is similar to highlighting text.

With the desired text selected, as I describe in the "Utilizing Highlights and Notes" section, earlier in this chapter, tap the Add Note button. A pop-up window appears with a text entry block and the onscreen keyboard. Type your notes using the keyboard and then tap Save.

Note that the text associated with your note is now highlighted in your book and is followed by a superscripted number. Tapping that number displays your note's text block — where you can edit or delete it.

You can view notes that other readers have made by turning on the Public Notes feature. Tap Menu⇨Settings⇨Reading Options⇨Notes & Highlights, and then turn on the toggle for Public Notes. See `https://kindle.amazon.com/faq` for more on public notes.

Viewing annotations

You can view all your notes, highlights, and bookmarks for a particular book. Tap Go To, and select the Notes tab from the menu that appears. Your notes, your highlights, and the popular and public highlights for that e-book are displayed.

You can also access your notes from a book by tapping the superscripted number, which opens that particular note. At the bottom of the note block, tap View Notes to display the same screen you accessed by using Go To. (The other options enable you to edit your note and, by tapping More, to delete or share the note.) To exit this screen, tap the X in the upper-right corner.

You can also view all your annotations across all your books, magazines, newspapers, and personal documents. Kindle Paperwhite places these in a My Clippings file that's available as a document from your Home screen. You can read your My Clippings file just as you would any other document on your Kindle Paperwhite.

You can view your annotations from a personal computer by going to `http://kindle.amazon.com` (United States and other countries) or `http://kindle.amazon.co.uk` (United Kingdom). Sign in and click the Your Highlights link.

Sharing notes and passages of interest

You probably noticed that when creating or viewing highlights and notes in your book, a Share button is available. This button lets you share a note and a link to the selected passage through Goodreads. If you've linked your Goodreads account to Facebook and Twitter, your notes will be shared on those sites, too. You can do all this directly from your Kindle Paperwhite — no computer required! The Share button is an easy way to let others know about books you're enjoying or passages you found interesting.

When you use your Kindle Paperwhite to share on Twitter, your tweet consists of your short note plus a Goodreads link to a list of quotes for the book you're reading. Figure 8-8 shows a sample tweet created on a Kindle Paperwhite.

Figure 8-8: Tweet a quote of interest from your Kindle Paperwhite.

From your Kindle Paperwhite, you can also update your Facebook status. An image of the book cover or a picture of the author (whatever is embedded in the book), an excerpt of highlighted text that you've selected, a note that you've written, and a link to the quote on Goodreads will be posted. Figure 8-9 shows a Facebook status update created from a Kindle Paperwhite.

Figure 8-9: A Facebook status update with a link to the book.

To take advantage of these features, you need to link your Kindle Paperwhite to Goodreads. Then you add Facebook and Twitter.

g   To begin tap the G (for Goodreads) icon on the toolbar. The screen shown in Figure 8-10 appears.

Figure 8-10: The screen you see when you select Goodreads for the first time.

If you already have a Goodreads account, tap Connect Existing Account. You can use your Facebook account, if you have one connected to Goodreads, or simply use your Goodreads credentials, as shown in Figure 8-11.

Figure 8-11: Connect using your Facebook account or Goodreads credentials.

If you don't have an existing account, tap Create New Account (refer to Figure 8-10). The screen shown in Figure 8-12 appears, asking you to create a Goodreads account with your Amazon credentials.

When you create your Goodreads account, you see screens that enable you to link to Facebook and Twitter. You can also make these connections later. To link or make changes to your Facebook account, you must go to Goodreads.com on your computer. To link to Twitter, follow these steps:

1. **Tap Menu➪Settings➪Reading Options.**

2. **Tap Social Networks. (If wireless is off, you're prompted to turn it on.)**

3. **Tap the Link Account button for Twitter.**

4. **Enter your Twitter e-mail address and your Twitter password on the authorization screen that appears.**

After your Kindle Paperwhite is linked, you can share a note about what you're reading by following these steps:

1. **From within a book, select text by tapping and holding down on a word, and then slide your finger across the page.**

2. **Tap the Share button.**

3. **Enter your message in the text box that appears.**

4. **Tap Share.**

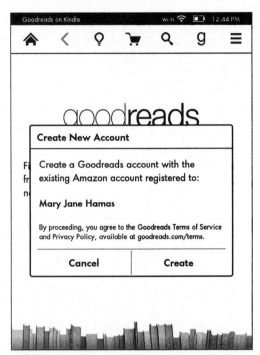

Figure 8-12: Create a Goodreads account with your Amazon credentials.

Your note and a link to the selected book passage posts to the accounts you've linked to your Kindle Paperwhite (Goodreads, Twitter, Facebook). All comments will be shared to Goodreads. You have the option of sharing to Twitter and Facebook by tapping to select (or deselect) the box in front of the Twitter and Facebook logos, as shown in Figure 8-13.

You can share Twitter and Facebook updates for periodicals and personal documents. Shared items appear on your Facebook wall (as a status update) and will be tweeted from your Twitter account. These comments will be linked to your page at `https://kindle.amazon.com/`. Comments that you share from periodicals and personal documents are not posted to Goodreads — Goodreads is exclusively for books.

When you finish a book, you can rate it and share it on Amazon and Goodreads. The Share page is shown in Figure 8-14.

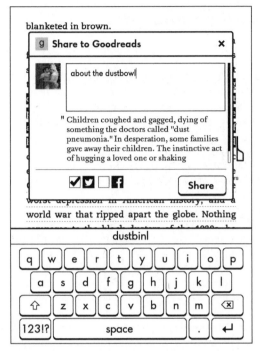

Figure 8-13: This comment will be shared on Goodreads and Twitter but not on Facebook.

Figure 8-14: Share and rate books on Amazon and Goodreads.

Playing with pictures

If the book you're reading has photographs and illustrations, you can see more information as well as make notes and marks. To begin, press and hold down (long-tap) on the photograph or illustration. A magnifying glass appears in the middle of the picture, and a box appears with Share, Add Note, Highlight, and More. These choices operate in the same way as discussed for words, notes, and highlights.

Tap the magnifying glass to enlarge the picture to full-screen size. If appropriate, the photo will rotate to landscape mode for best viewing. Tap the picture again to return to your book.

Would you like to make a screenshot from your Kindle Paperwhite? It's easy! On the desired page, place your thumbs lightly in the upper-right and lower-left corners, and press simultaneously. The screen will blink. Use the USB cable to attach your Kindle Paperwhite to your computer. The screenshot is listed in the root directory. From there you can copy or move the picture to your hard drive, rename it, save it, and use it however you want.

Note that the double-thumbpress maneuver takes a bit of practice. If your desired screenshot doesn't appear the first time, just try again.

Viewing with X-Ray

Some books have the X-ray feature enabled. This feature provides a view into recurring items: characters, settings, topics, and phrases that occur throughout the book. You can view this information for the current page, the current chapter, or the entire book.

Tap the top of the screen to display the toolbar, and then tap X-Ray to see a screen like the one shown in Figure 8-15. (Note that if the X-ray feature is not enabled for the book you're reading, the option will appear dimmed.) Tap any term to view additional information from Wikipedia (if enabled) and to see the other locations in the book where that term appears.

Going a Little Further with Goodreads

As discussed, you can share quotes and short comments from Paperwhite to Goodreads, Facebook, and Twitter. But Goodreads offers much more for voracious readers. You can use shelves to organize your books by those you have read, are currently reading, and want to read. You can connect with friends who have similar reading interests to discover new books. And the Updates feature enables you to see what your friends are reading and view their comments and ratings.

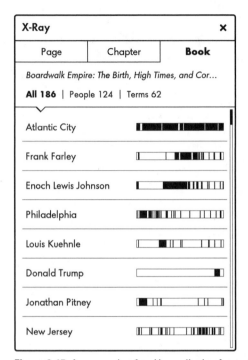

Figure 8-15: An example of an X-ray display from a book about Atlantic City.

One particularly useful feature is the capability to add books from your Amazon Cloud account to Goodreads. With the Goodreads app open, select Add Amazon Books (in the upper right). The screen shown in Figure 8-16 appears. From here, you can add books to Goodreads, either by rating or by adding the book to a shelf.

If you're familiar with Goodreads, you will find that the Goodreads app has much of the functionality that has been available on mobile apps and PCs. If you're new to Goodreads, take time to play with it and discover what you can do. It can be a great tool for organizing your library and keeping track of what you've read, as well as connecting with other readers and friends.

Using Whispersync with Kindle Editions and Audible Books

Prior versions of the Kindle e-reader included audio capabilities which allowed you to listen to a book on your device or use Text-to-Speech to have a book read to you. The Kindle Paperwhite does not include these features, but don't despair — you can still listen to a book and have it sync with the Kindle edition on your Kindle Paperwhite by using Whispersync for Voice.

Figure 8-16: Adding books from your Amazon collection to Goodreads.

To begin, you will need the following:

- ✔ **A Kindle Paperwhite:** Make sure that Whispersync is turned on at your Amazon account. Go to www.amazon.com/myk and select Manage Your Devices. Device Synchronization is near the bottom of the page.

- ✔ **A device that plays audio files and supports the Audible application:** The Audible application is designed to play books purchased from Audible.com or Audible books purchased from Amazon.

- ✔ **The Kindle Edition of a book and the Audible audiobook version:** You need to search on Amazon to find Kindle books with Audible counterparts. If a book supports Whispersync for Voice, that fact will be noted on the product page, as shown in Figure 8-17.

Amazon offers special promotions on Kindle Edition/Audible book combos. When you buy a Kindle book, check to see whether the Audible book is available at a discounted price.

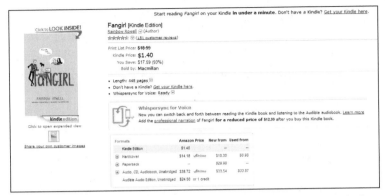

Figure 8-17: A Whispersync for Voice edition is also available, as shown in the middle of the page.

Now all you need to do is begin reading (or listening). When you switch devices, the synchronization should be automatic. See Figure 8-18 for an illustration of the sync screen on your Kindle Paperwhite and Figure 8-19 for the screen on the audio device, in this case, an iPhone. If the sync does not happen automatically, tap Menu➪Sync to Furthest Page Read.

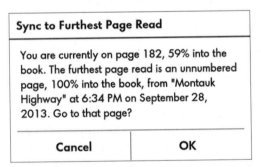

Figure 8-18: Synchronization screen on a Kindle Paperwhite.

You do not need to purchase the two books at the same time to have them synchronize between the Kindle edition and audiobook. Books bought at different times will still sync.

At the time of this writing, the synchronization feature was available only between Amazon Kindle Editions and audiobooks purchased from Audible.com, which is an Amazon company.

The Fault in Our Stars (Unabridged)

You are currently at location 5:21:58. The last heard location across all your devices is 7:13:35. Go to that location?

| Cancel | OK |

Figure 8-19: Synchronization screen on an audio device.

Accessing the Experimental Browser

Yes indeed, your Kindle Paperwhite sports a built-in browser that you can use to access the Internet. The browser isn't full-featured like the one you surf with on your computer, but it is a usable, albeit stripped-down, browser that you can take advantage of when you're out somewhere with your Kindle Paperwhite and need to get online in a hurry.

If you have a Kindle Paperwhite 3G, free web browsing in 3G mode is limited. You can access only the Amazon website (including the Kindle Store, of course!) and Wikipedia via 3G wireless. For accessing other websites, you need to use a Wi-Fi connection.

Although the Kindle Paperwhite's web browser is simple, it does offer some compelling features. Here are some of my favorite things about the Kindle Paperwhite web browser:

- ✔ Even though web access is limited under 3G wireless, this access is free. (Most devices other than Kindles that use 3G require an access fee or monthly charges.) You can access Amazon or Wikipedia anytime and anywhere with your Kindle Paperwhite 3G — as long as you're in an area covered by the AT&T cellular data network used by the Kindle Paperwhite.

✔ The web browser provides a convenient way to connect to the web any time you're in a Wi-Fi hotspot. This hotspot could be your own home wireless network or the Wi-Fi available in a coffee shop or an airport, for example. (*Note:* Some hotspots charge a fee for Internet connectivity.)

✔ The Kindle Paperwhite's web browser enables you to immediately jump to websites from links provided in e-books, blogs, or other content.

✔ For simple, text-oriented sites, such as mobile versions of most websites, the convenience of having web access available from your Kindle Paperwhite can be a timesaver.

Conversely, the rudimentary nature of the Kindle Paperwhite web browser has some drawbacks, including these:

✔ The Kindle Paperwhite's grayscale display is less than ideal for most web browsing. If you're accessing sites that are rich in graphics and colors, you'll have a less appealing experience.

✔ The web browser doesn't support websites that use Flash or Shockwave multimedia effects.

✔ Java applets aren't supported. Some websites use Java applets for animations or to provide complex functionality.

✔ Videos are not playable through the web browser.

✔ The web browser may be unavailable in some countries outside the United States.

Getting online

To access the web browser, tap the Menu icon from the Home screen and then tap the Experimental Browser option, as shown in Figure 8-20.

The first time you launch the browser, the default Yahoo! screen appears. Tap Menu⇨Bookmarks to display the default list of website bookmarks. Amazon is at the top, followed by Wikipedia, Google, and the *New York Times.* Tap one of the bookmarks to open the bookmarked page in the browser. If you leave the browser and later return, the last page you viewed will open by default.

You can open the browser also by tapping any web address link from content that you read on your Kindle Paperwhite, such as a book or a blog.

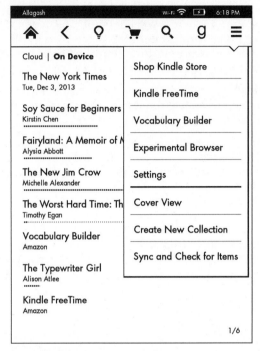

Figure 8-20: Access Amazon's Experimental browser from the Menu icon.

Browsing basics

Your Kindle Paperwhite web browser displays the web address, or URL, in its address bar for the last web page you accessed. To change that URL or enter a new one, tap the address bar and use the onscreen keyboard to enter your desired URL. Tap the arrow to the right to navigate to the site.

 When entering the URL, you can leave out the `http://` prefix and the www part of the address. For example, you can type **cnn.com** rather than **http://www.cnn.com**.

 On web pages that have more content than can fit on one displayed page, a scroll bar appears on the right side of the browser. You can drag your finger around the page to scroll up and down to view more of the page.

You can use bookmarks to save frequently used web pages and to avoid reentering long URLs from the Kindle Paperwhite's onscreen keyboard. Here are the essentials for working with web browser bookmarks:

✔ **Adding a bookmark:** Tap Menu⇨Bookmark This Page.

✔ **Accessing your saved bookmarks:** From the web browser, tap Menu⇨Bookmarks. Use this method to access the sample bookmarks that Amazon has preloaded on your Kindle Paperwhite as well.

✔ **Deleting a bookmark:** Tap Remove at the bottom of the bookmarks screen. A check box appears for each displayed bookmark. Tap the check box for one or more bookmarks, and then tap Remove.

✔ **Editing a bookmark:** Tap Edit at the bottom of the bookmarks screen. Tap a bookmark to edit its name.

Given the nature of the Kindle Paperwhite's display size, you'll probably want to zoom in on areas of a web page. Unpinch on the display to zoom in, and pinch to zoom out. (See Chapter 3 for more on how to navigate the Kindle Paperwhite's touchscreen.) When the page is zoomed in, you can pan around the web page by swiping your finger across the display.

Special settings

You usually don't have to be concerned about the default settings of your Kindle Paperwhite's web browser. However, situations may arise in which tinkering with the settings can resolve problems and improve the speed of browsing from one page to another.

You can see the available options from any web page by tapping Menu⇨Browser Settings. The following options are available:

✔ **Clear History:** Your Kindle Paperwhite saves the URLs and content from web pages you've visited previously, to speed up load times when you visit those pages again. Use the Clear History option to delete this saved information.

✔ **Clear Cookies:** Some web pages save small strings of information, or *cookies,* on your Kindle Paperwhite's hard drive. Cookies can be used, for example, to save your login information so you don't have to reenter it on each page of a site. Use the Clear Cookies option to delete this information. You may want to do this if your web browser doesn't respond or responds very slowly.

✔ **Disable JavaScript:** Many websites use JavaScript to provide enhanced functionality, such as submenus that appear dynamically when a main menu option is selected. If you find that the web browser responds slowly, try using this option to disable JavaScript.

✔ **Disable Images:** Depending on the speed of your Internet connection, web page graphics and pictures can be slow to load. You can choose to eliminate the images and view only the text content of web pages by selecting the Disable Images option.

Some web pages have *articles,* which are defined areas that can make reading a web page easier. For example, news sites often organize their content into articles to define sections of text and graphics that belong together. You can view articles more conveniently by tapping Menu⇨Article Mode. Your Kindle Paperwhite's web browser will now filter the content it displays to the desired article's text and images.

Article Mode works well with many news sites. When viewing the article, swipe the display to scroll up or down. To turn off Article Mode, tap Menu⇨Web Mode.

Chapter 9

Kindles for Kids and Students

In This Chapter

▶ Assessing a child's readiness for a Kindle

▶ Nurturing a love of reading in children

▶ Kindling for students at all education levels

*W*hen the Kindle was first released in 2007, it was expensive and available books were limited primarily to novels — thus it was considered by many to be a device for adult readers, not children and students. Since then, much has changed and the Kindle is widely adopted in schools and colleges. Young readers own their own Kindles and tote them to camp, school, and sleepovers. For many children who have resisted reading, owning a Kindle has changed their outlook and truly "Kindled" a new love for books.

This chapter introduces you to the world of Kindles and kids. If you are a parent wondering about whether to buy a Kindle for your child, read on. In addition, school innovations are briefly discussed. If you are a teacher, maybe some of the information here will fire your imagination and encourage you to learn more.

This book is specifically about the Kindle Paperwhite, but many schools and colleges use other Kindle devices, including the Kindle Fire, which is the Android tablet device of the Kindle family. A full discussion of all alternatives and opportunities is beyond the scope of this chapter, but it does provide a good starting point for all who are interested in Kindle usage with their children and students.

Is Kindle Right for Your Child?

You've bought a Kindle Paperwhite and love the e-ink screen and built-in light. You want to buy one for your child. Before you do so, consider the following factors:

✔ **Age:** The Kindle Paperwhite is a grayscale device, so it is not ideal for young children reading pictures books. In addition, young children won't understand that the Kindle Paperwhite is breakable and needs to be handled with care. As a general rule, if a child is reading chapter books, he or she is probably old enough to handle a Kindle Paperwhite safely.

If you have a Kindle Fire, you might investigate using that to read picture books to a young child. Also, the Paperwhite's built-in light makes it the perfect device to use when reading chapter books and beloved favorites aloud at bedtime. Don't be afraid to experiment and see what your child enjoys.

Many reading experts suggest reading books to your children slightly above their current reading level. You can discuss new words and concepts and use the dictionary to look up definitions.

✔ **Track record with electronic devices:** Following on the preceding bullet point, how has your child fared with electronic devices in the past? Has he or she dropped, broken, or lost them? The front of the Kindle Paperwhite is about 95 percent screen and can be easily broken. Keep this in mind as you consider a purchase for your child.

✔ **Interest in reading:** The case studies about the success rate of Kindles in schools would lead you to believe that all children magically become avid readers once the device is placed in their hands. I am sure that the novelty of the device does intrigue many children and encourage them to read. At the same time, parental involvement is also part of successfully using a Kindle to encourage a reluctant reader to become more engaged with books. Note that many educators consider children aged 7 to 11 to be at the ideal age to develop a lifelong love of reading. A marker for readiness is the transition from picture books to chapter books.

Remember that our children are digital natives and have grown up with technology. They take to it more easily than those of us who are (ahem!) a bit older.

If you decide to go ahead and purchase a Kindle for your child, remember the following points:

- **Protective covers:** Buy a protective cover and encourage your child to use it. As noted, Kindles are fragile and need to be treated with care. If your child prefers to read the device out of a cover, make sure he or she has some sort of protective envelope or sleeve for storage during nonreading times. A wide variety of covers and other paraphernalia are discussed in Chapter 10.

- **Backpack packing:** Even with a cover, a Kindle Paperwhite could be crushed or damaged if tossed carelessly in a backpack with a load of heavy books. Look through your child's backpack with him or her and designate a specific pocket as its "home" to be used when the backpack is carried.

- **Kindle at school or camp:** If your child hopes to take her Kindle to school or camp (or somewhere else), take a few minutes to contact the administrator and make sure this is okay. Policies vary widely and change frequently. The use of personal electronic devices, such as Kindles, may be discouraged or prohibited due to issues of theft or competition among children. On the other hand, a school may have a Kindle program in place but not enough devices for all students — and the teachers would be thrilled to have your child bring his or her own device. You'll never know unless you ask.

  You can also be an advocate for Kindle use in your child's school. If the administrators or teachers are not familiar with the device and how it can be used, take advantage of this teachable moment! Let them know how much you enjoy your Kindle Paperwhite and why you think it would enhance the learning environment in their classrooms. The National PTA has a variety of resources for encouraging the use of Kindles at home and at school — this is discussed a bit later in this chapter.

Using Parental Controls

When you buy a Kindle for your child, it will be registered to your Amazon account. Your child will have access to the Kindle Store to make purchases as well as being able to view and download books in the Cloud. The Kindle's experimental web browser and the Goodreads app (see Chapter 8) are also accessible. You can restrict your child's access to all four by using parental controls.

To access parental controls, tap Menu⇨Settings⇨Device Options⇨Parental Controls⇨Restrictions. The screen shown in Figure 9-1 appears. Tap the toggle switch for Web Browser, Kindle Store, Cloud, or Goodreads to restrict access. You'll be asked to enter a password, as shown in Figure 9-2. Input a hint to help you remember your password.

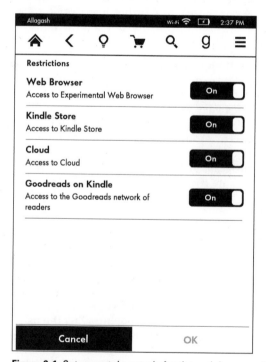

Figure 9-1: Set parental controls for the web browser, the Kindle Store, the Cloud, and Goodreads.

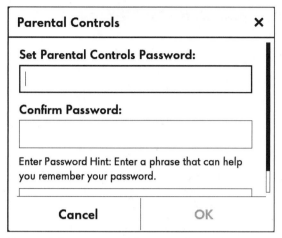

Figure 9-2: Set a password for parental controls.

Note that when access to the web, store, or Cloud is restricted with parental controls, you will not be able to deregister your Kindle Paperwhite, nor will you be able to update the software running the device unless you use the password to unlock the device. The Shopping Cart and Goodreads icons are also dimmed, as shown in Figure 9-3.

Parental controls affect only the local Kindle on which they are enabled. Other Kindles on your account can still access the Cloud, Goodreads, the Kindle Store, and the Kindle web browser.

Only you can decide if you need to use parental controls for your child's Kindle. When these controls are on, your child cannot sample content, download free books, or borrow books from the Kindle Owners' Library (if you have Amazon Prime). On the other hand, without parental controls, your child has free rein to buy things from the store — on your credit card — and can see and download books in the Cloud. You need to weigh these alternatives to make the best decision.

Figure 9-3: Note that shopping, the experimental browser, and Goodreads appear dimmed when parental controls are turned on.

Igniting a Love of Reading

As noted earlier, just putting a Kindle in a child's hands is probably not going to turn him or her into an avid reader overnight. However, you can take advantage of certain Kindle features to help nurture a reading interest and make it flourish into an enjoyable hobby and lifelong habit.

Make reading fun

Encourage your children to take advantage of the various features of the Kindle Paperwhite to personalize their device and make reading fun. Show them how to change the font, font size, line spacing, and margins to customize the screen for the best reading experience. Show them how to adjust the light for different lighting conditions. Take advantage of the teachable moment to explain why you want a brighter light in a brightly lit area versus a dimmer light in low light conditions. (If *you* don't remember why, see Chapter 3).

Aa Remember, you change the font, font size, line spacing, and margins from the same menu. Tap at the top of the screen, and then tap the icon shown in the margin to display the Fonts menu, shown in Figure 9-4.

Dictionary and X-ray are powerful features that can also spur an interest in reading. Children are often discouraged by reading because they don't understand the words or are confused by locations and characters. Teach them how easy it is to look up a word by simply long-tapping — the dictionary will open and display the definition. X-ray is helpful as a refresher of characters and places, as shown in Figure 9-5.

Translation is another feature that children find intriguing. From the dictionary page, tap More, and then tap Translation. Remember that the Kindle Paperwhite can provide translations of a word into 16 languages, from Chinese to Spanish. Give your child a challenge: Choose a common word, such as *Thanks,* and translate it into several languages. Which ones are similar? Which ones are different? Which ones don't even look like English?

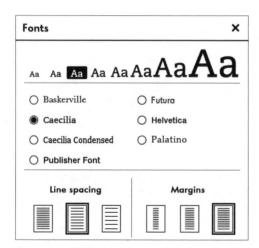

Figure 9-4: Adjust the font, font size, line spacing, and margins all from the same menu.

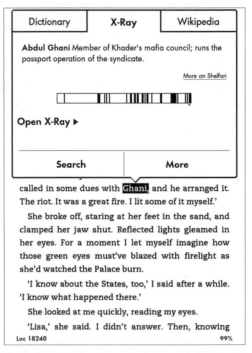

Figure 9-5: Use X-ray to remind yourself of who a character is in a novel.

Vocabulary Builder

Remember that every time a word is accessed in the dictionary, it is added to a running list of words in Vocabulary Builder. Within a book, this list is accessed by tapping Menu➪Vocabulary Builder. Show your child how to sort the list by word or by book. Have your child tap Flashcards to practice a definition and see the word used in context, and then tap Mark as Mastered to remove the word from the Flashcard list. For more detail on Vocabulary Builder, see Chapter 8.

Kindle Free Time

The Kindle Free Time application, which is available for the Kindle Fire and Kindle Paperwhite, allows you to create individual profiles for your children and customize a reading goal of minutes per day with badges and rewards. As a parent, you can access a progress report that lets you see the total time spent reading, badges earned, and books finished.

Kindle Free Time lets you designate books your child can access from your Cloud at Amazon. Kindle Free Time is activated when you set a password for parental controls. To access parental controls, tap Menu⇨Settings⇨Device Options⇨Parental Controls. Tap Kindle Free Time and the screen shown in Figure 9-6 appears. Follow the on screen instructions to add a profile for your children. You can add books from the Cloud to their individual profiles.

When reading in Kindle Free Time, the Goodreads icon on the toolbar is replaced by a badge. Tap the badge to access a variety of goals, such as Book Worm (30 minutes of reading) or Super Book Worm (reading 30 minutes a day for 7 days).

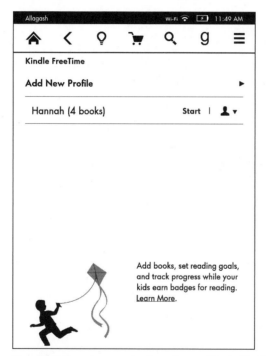

Figure 9-6: Create customized reading profiles in Kindle Free Time.

While in Kindle Free Time, a number of features are blocked:

- Browsing and purchasing in the Kindle Store
- Access to the experimental web browser
- Access to Wikipedia
- Social sharing on Facebook, Goodreads, and Twitter

In some ways, Kindle Free Time mimics parental controls (discussed previously). However, Kindle Free Time blocks these features only when Kindle Free Time is turned on and a child is reading within his or her profile. When Kindle Free Time is exited — which must be done by reentering the password you selected — these features are reactivated.

After Kindle Free Time has been activated on your Kindle, it appears as a menu choice on your Home screen, as shown in Figure 9-7. It also becomes a menu choice when you tap the Menu icon, as shown in Figure 9-8.

In-line footnotes

Older children may read books with footnotes. The Kindle Paperwhite makes it much easier to look up footnotes than earlier versions of the device. Simply tap the superscripted number or the footnote mark to open the page in Footnote, as shown in Figure 9-9. To exit the footnote, tap the X in the upper-right corner. To read all the footnotes in a book, tap Go to Footnotes.

Figure 9-7: Kindle Free Time appears as an option on the Home screen.

Allagash
Wi-Fi
3:14 PM
Cloud | On Device
kindle FreeTime
Shop Kindle Store
Kindle FreeTime
Vocabulary Builder
Experimental Browser
Settings
List View
Create New Collection
Sync and Check for Items
Award-Winning Books
ENDER'S GAME
ORSON SCOTT CARD
SPEAKER FOR THE DEAD
ORSON SCOTT CARD
ROUND HOUSE

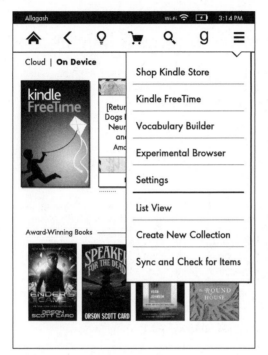

Figure 9-8: Kindle Free Time appears as a menu choice

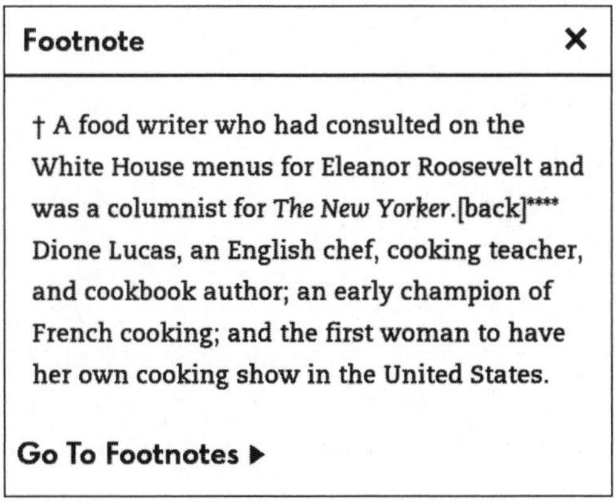

Footnote
×
† A food writer who had consulted on the White House menus for Eleanor Roosevelt and was a columnist for *The New Yorker*.[back]**** Dione Lucas, an English chef, cooking teacher, and cookbook author; an early champion of French cooking; and the first woman to have her own cooking show in the United States.
Go To Footnotes ▶

Figure 9-9: Accessing a footnote without leaving the page of a book.

More tips to encourage a love of reading

The National PTA has teamed up with Amazon to promote reading and has selected the Kindle as its official e-reader. They offer the following tips to encourage a love of reading in all children (adapted from National PTA, `https://images-na.ssl-images-amazon.com/images/G/01/kindle/pta/pta-tips-download.pdf`):

- **Encourage reading in your home.** Set an example by reading in front of your child both for pleasure and practicality. Create a special place in your home where you can read together.

- **Spend 30 minutes each day reading together.** When reading with your child, ask him or her to describe what is going on in the scene or happening in the story.

- **Sign up your child for a library card.** You can borrow books from the library for Kindle using OverDrive, but you must have a library card to do so. A library card also lets your child borrow books the old-fashioned way.

- **Attend a library event.** Look for a schedule of story times and author readings — most libraries host these types of events weekly or monthly.

- **Become involved at your child's school.** Communicate with teachers to monitor your child's progress. Ask what you can do at home to support your child's reading.

- **Applaud your child for reading.** Reward your child for reading a certain number of books or finishing a challenging book. Kindle Free Time allows you to monitor progress and recognize achievements.

- **Give books as presents.** Give books as a gift, especially on topics your child enjoys. It's easy to gift books for the Kindle Paperwhite — see Chapter 6.

- **Help your child write his or her own stories.** Encourage your child to write stories based on his or her experiences or favorite characters from other books, movies, or TV shows.

- **Make flashcards to learn new words.** Vocabulary Builder is ideal for this task!

- **Take your child to the eye doctor.** Schedule an eye exam to ensure that any vision problems are promptly addressed.

Be creative with content

Keep reading fun for your child by encouraging a variety of books — nothing kills a burgeoning love of reading faster than getting stuck with a stack of boring books! At that same time, you want to protect your wallet. Take advantage of the many free deals and bargain-priced books that Amazon offers. Hundreds of free out-of-copyright classics can be obtained from Amazon and other sources, such as Project Gutenberg (`www.gutenberg.org/`).

Amazon has a weekly e-mail list through its Amazon Delivers program specifically for books for children at a variety of ages. Editors select new and trending books, as well as exclusive content and theme-oriented booklists. To learn more or subscribe, check out the following:

- **Children 3–5 years:** www.amazon.com/gp/gss/detail/23595880

- **Children 6–8 years:** www.amazon.com/gp/gss/detail/23596100

- **Children 9–12 years:** www.amazon.com/gp/gss/detail/23597260

- **Teens and young adults:** www.amazon.com/gp/gss/detail/21546200/

- **All Amazon subscriptions:** www.amazon.com/gp/gss/browse/17820

Don't forget borrowing

Not all content has to be purchased. If you're an Amazon Prime member, take advantage of the Kindle Owners' Lending Library, which is discussed in detail in Chapter 6. Remember that only one book per month can be borrowed from the Kindle Owners' Lending Library *per account* under this program. If you have multiple Kindles on your account, you may want to devise a plan so that everyone has equal access to the library. Alternatively, you may decide that your child can take advantage of one free book every month. Keep in mind that thousands of books are available through this program.

Your local library is another reliable source of books to borrow. More than 11,000 libraries in the United States have Kindle books available to loan. To find a library in your area, go to http://search.overdrive.com/ and select Library Search. After you identify a library for borrowing, you'll need to contact it for a library card (if you don't already have one) and a PIN.

To find a book of interest, search your selected library's website. Available books will be displayed. If a book is currently checked out, you can place a hold to receive the book when it is available. Follow the online instructions to borrow and receive the book. Library books must be delivered via Wi-Fi, not 3G. Some library books must be downloaded by connecting your Kindle Paperwhite to your computer with the USB cable.

Library books are available for a fixed period of time, depending on the policy of your selected library. Amazon will send you a reminder e-mail three days before the book is due to be returned. If you want to return a book earlier than its due date, go to Manage Your Kindle (www.amazon.com/myk), find the book in your Cloud, and select the option to return it.

Borrowing books from public libraries is presently available only in the United States.

Amazon has a two-minute video on borrowing books from the library. You can watch it at www.amazon.com/gp/help/customer/display.html/?nodeId=200747550.

Kindle on Campus

Sending your child to school with his or her Kindle (if allowed) is a great way to encourage reading during quiet time and designated reading periods, but it doesn't have to be an individual experience. Many teachers and librarians throughout the country are exploring innovative ways to incorporate Kindles and other reading devices into their classrooms and curricula.

Whispercast

Amazon has a number of case studies that demonstrate how the Kindle is being used to develop a passion for reading and increase student literacy. You can read more at www.amazon.com/gp/feature.html?docId=1000412651.

Central to many of these programs is Whispercast, a free online program that allows schools (and businesses) to manage Kindles and distribute Kindle content to the devices registered to the master Whispercast account. An organization can sign up for Whispercast at https://whispercast.amazon.com/signup/.

Whispercast streamlines the process of sending Kindle content to readers registered to the account. Books, apps, and other materials can be managed from a central account and sent to all users on the account or selected groups. For example, Clearwater High School in Pinellas County, Florida, provided 3,628 Kindles to students in the 9th through 12th grades, and Whispercast is being used to manage the content requirements for these students. Teachers are finding new ways to use the Kindles by downloading handouts, study guides, and documents such as the U.S. Constitution. Administrators note that students are reading more, and students appreciate the lightened load in their backpacks, with many books on a single device.

The video at www.youtube.com/watch?v=SQOv1c7sQ20 provides a nice overview of Whispercast in action at two schools.

National PTA

In 2013, the National PTA teamed up with Amazon and adopted the Kindle as its national e-reader. They've developed a variety of learning programs and pedagogical materials that can be used at the local level to encourage and support reading in school and at home. "The PTA Family Reading Experience, Powered by Kindle" focuses on improving the reading skills of children between kindergarten and fifth grade. Activities are designed to be fun and engaging, while addressing the five domains of reading: phonological awareness, phonics, fluency, comprehension, and vocabulary. To learn more and download activity guides in English and Spanish, visit www.pta.org/familyreading.

For college students

Amazon has a number of features and promotions for college students, although not all of them are Kindle-based. For example, Amazon Student allows college students to sign up for a free six-month trial of Amazon Prime, which provides free two-day shipping on all purchases, including textbooks. After six months, the cost is $39/year (50 percent off the regular price) — after this kicks in, the program includes access to instant streaming videos and TV episodes, as well as access to the Kindle Owners' Lending Library.

Textbooks are available for the Kindle in several disciplines, such as accounting, art history, economics, mathematics, nursing, philosophy, and science. Texts are being added daily — check frequently to see if there are textbooks that apply to your studies.

In many textbooks, enhanced features such as X-Ray for Textbooks and Notebook are best viewed and used on a full-color device such as the Kindle Fire HD. In fact, you may not even be able to download a sample or purchase a textbook for the Kindle Paperwhite. Check at the product page for the book you are interested in to see what devices are available for delivery. Note that many textbooks can be viewed on various devices, such as the iPad, Android tablet, laptop, or Mac using the Kindle for Reading App. This app is free — see Chapter 4 for more details.

Textbooks can be sampled, purchased, or rented. Renting offers a cheaper alternative to purchasing a book, as noted in the "Renting Kindle books" sidebar. All textbooks, no matter how acquired, can be returned within seven days for a full refund.

Renting Kindle books

Amazon now enables you to rent a textbook in Kindle format. Books can be rented for a specific time period, usually between 30 and 360 days. Books that are available for rental have the Rent This Book designation on the product page.

If you decide you want to buy a rented book, your rental fee will be applied to the purchase price. However, you must purchase the book during the rental period; after the rental has expired, you lose the rental credit and need to pay full price to purchase the book.

When the rental expires, the book will no longer be available on your Kindle Paperwhite (or another device on which you may be reading the book). However, if you've made notes and highlights in the book, these will be saved in your account at Amazon.

Rental books can be returned for a full refund within 7 days of rental, the same as with any Kindle book purchase. This policy is helpful for students who decide to drop a class and no longer need the book. What if a student chooses a 90-day rental and then needs the book for only 30 days? Unfortunately, Amazon does not provide partial refunds.

To learn more, go to Kindle Support at www.amazon.com/gp/help/customer/display.html/ and search for *Renting Kindle Books*.

Chapter 10

Accessorizing

In This Chapter

▶ Dressing up and protecting your Kindle Paperwhite
▶ Adding external accessories
▶ Insuring your Kindle Paperwhite

Kindle Paperwhite accessories come in hundreds of varieties and colors. You can use a skin, screen protector, or cover to protect your Kindle Paperwhite, but these accessories can also be fashion statements. Accessorize your Kindle Paperwhite and give it your own personal pizzazz.

In this chapter, I discuss an assortment of accessories, including vinyl skins, covers, and bags, plus lights, styli, plugs, adapters, and stands. I wrap up the chapter with a brief discussion of damage protection policies from Amazon and third-party sources.

Adding the First Layer

When you buy a Kindle Paperwhite, it ships in a simple box with a USB cable and a card of instructions. That's it! Many people like to read the Kindle Paperwhite as is, right out of the box. But if you want to hide smudges and dirt while dressing up your device, a skin serves well as the first layer. To protect your Kindle Paperwhite from scratches, check out screen protectors. Is either essential? No, but that doesn't detract from their popularity!

Vinyl skins

One of the major complaints of the first-generation Kindle was that it looked old-fashioned and bulky. Many people didn't care for the off-white case. The solution? *Vinyl skins,* which are like a second skin and have been produced for all versions of Kindle e-readers.

Because they're vinyl, skins adhere to the device without glue or adhesive. Skin makers have responded to the demand with an astonishing array of designs.

Some Kindle Paperwhite owners have reported that the black bezel shows fingerprints and smudges much more readily than earlier models. A skin is the ideal solution for this issue.

The skin comes in two pieces for the front (with a cutout for the screen) and the back. To apply the skin, peel the vinyl from the backing sheet, place it on the Kindle Paperwhite in the correct place, and smooth out any air bubbles. That's it!

Keep in mind the following hints to make skin application as effortless as possible:

- ✓ **Take your time.** Give yourself a few minutes to apply a skin. Don't try to do it when you're in a hurry.

- ✓ **Use a clean and well lit work surface.**

- ✓ **Wash your hands.** You don't want to leave smudges or fingerprints on the skin. Also, oil from your skin could make the vinyl not adhere as well.

- ✓ **Clean the Kindle Paperwhite surface before applying the skin.** Don't use solvents or cleaners on the device. Just rub the front bezel and back clean with a soft cloth.

- ✓ **Adhere the back piece first.** The large back piece is easier to work with than the front. After you get the knack of placing a skin, adhere the front piece on the bezel surrounding the screen.

People with small, delicate hands usually have an easier time applying a skin. If that's not you, consider asking someone with smaller hands for help.

If you buy a skin from DecalGirl, the piece for the back of the Kindle Paperwhite is a perfect fit for the inside of the Amazon cover. This might be a colorful option to dress up the inside front cover if you don't plan on taking your Kindle Paperwhite out of its Amazon case.

The skin can be removed easily for repositioning while you're applying it but becomes semi-permanent after it's on for a few hours. If you decide to change the skin, you can pull it off easily after you work an edge free, but it's likely to stretch out of shape. Although some people have been able to reuse a skin after an initial application, plan on using it only once.

Some people have had success reshaping a skin that has been removed from a Kindle Paperwhite by using a hair dryer on the warm setting.

The following are some advantages of a vinyl skin:

- ✔ **Decoration:** For a small investment of approximately $9–$30, you can change the look of your Kindle Paperwhite as the spirit moves you.

- ✔ **Free of dirt and finger smudges:** If the skin gets dirty, you can easily take it off and replace it. Cleaning the Kindle Paperwhite case is a little trickier because you don't want cleaning solution to accidentally seep into the screen around the bezel.

A number of skin manufacturers exist, and many sell their products on Amazon. The following are three of the most popular retailers of vinyl skins with designs for the Kindle Paperwhite:

- ✔ **DecalGirl** (`www.decalgirlcom`): One of the first out of the gate with skins for the original Kindle, DecalGirl sells its skins on Amazon and on its website. Choose from hundreds of designs in a matte or shiny finish or design your own for a reasonable price.

- ✔ **GelaSkins** (`www.gelaskins.com`): Another popular manufacturer with skins sold through its website, GelaSkins features one-of-a-kind designs from up-and-coming as well as established artists. The company also allows you to use your own photos or art to create custom skins.

- ✔ **iStyles** (`www.istyles.com`): Based in Singapore, this company creates vinyl skins for many devices. You can pay in U.S. dollars, euros, British pounds, or Singapore dollars and have your skin shipped worldwide. Skin prices are comparable to those of U.S. manufacturers and shipping costs are reasonable.

Skins aren't just for the Kindle family of e-readers. All the manufacturers listed here make skins for a variety of devices, including laptops, smartphones, and gaming consoles.

Screen protectors

Screen protectors are just what the name implies — a plastic covering for the screen to keep it safe from scratches and smudges. Users have mixed opinions regarding whether they're necessary. On one hand, the screen is the most delicate part of the Kindle Paperwhite, and although you can wipe off a smudge, a scratch is permanent. A screen protector can be an inexpensive way to provide a layer of security for your device. On the other hand, screen protectors can be tough to apply and can obscure the screen, making reading more difficult. Because the Kindle Paperwhite is all about reading, having something that may interfere with that pastime isn't a bonus.

Keep in mind that the Kindle Paperwhite is a touchscreen device. You do need to put your fingers on the screen to turn the page, look up words in the dictionary, or buy e-books from the Kindle Store. The screen will get dirty. Plus, you may splash milk on it while eating a bowl of cereal or sneeze on it. I leave the decision of whether the screen protector is necessary up to you.

The following companies offer screen protectors:

- ✔ **BoxWave** (`www.boxwave.com`): This company offers two screen protectors, one with an anti-glare feature and a second with crystal-clear viewing. It also offers the Screen Puff, an ultrapuffy screen wiper, available in seven colors — you can coordinate with your cover and skin!

- ✔ **M-Edge** (`www.medgestore.com`): Visit this company for a two-pack of screen protectors, plus a cleaning cloth.

- ✔ **Great Shield:** Get a three-pack of screen protectors from this company by going to `www.amazon.com/GreatShield-Anti-Glare-Protector-Paperwhite-Keyboard/dp/B004JWA70I`.

When searching for screen protectors, make sure to specify the Kindle Paperwhite or a 6-inch screen device. Screen protectors for the Kindle Touch will fit the Kindle Paperwhite because they both have 6-inch screens. Protectors for earlier versions of the Kindle, however, will not fit the Kindle Paperwhite screen.

Covering Your Device

If you want to buy only one add-on for your Kindle Paperwhite, I suggest a cover, a sleeve, an envelope, or a jacket because it will protect your Kindle Paperwhite, particularly the screen, from damage. Although nothing is foolproof, having the screen covered when the Kindle Paperwhite isn't in use is a good idea.

Following is a description of these essential add-ons:

- **Cover:** In general, a Kindle Paperwhite cover is kept on the device at all times, even while reading. Most covers fold back for reading and close with a snap, a buckle, a magnet, or an elastic cord.

- **Sleeve:** Neoprene sleeves are usually close fitting and may have a zipper closure. Some users who opt not to use a cover protect their Kindle Paperwhite in a sleeve.

- **Envelope:** Similar to a sleeve but not quite as form-fitting, an envelope is another option for readers who prefer to use their Kindle Paperwhite without a cover.

- **Jacket:** A jacket is like a bag or suit for your Kindle Paperwhite. The device goes inside, and the jacket is secured with a zipper. Some jackets are clear vinyl to provide protection while reading near water or in dusty areas.

Covers, sleeves, envelopes, and jackets are among the most popular Kindle Paperwhite accessories, so you can choose from plenty of options.

Covers galore!

Kindle Paperwhite covers are available in a variety of materials, from fabric to leather to neoprene, at prices ranging from less than $20 to more than $200. To get a sense of the variety out there, go to Amazon (www.amazon.com) and choose Kindle⇨Accessories from the navigation menu at the left. On the page that appears, you'll see covers featured prominently.

Securing the device

Most covers are secured to the Kindle Paperwhite by using one of the following options:

- **Tabs:** Simply slip the Kindle Paperwhite under the tab in each corner to hold it in place. Covers from Belkin, M-Edge, and Oberon are popular examples of covers that use tabs.

   Oberon Design, a small family-owned business based in Santa Rosa, California, makes hand-tooled leather covers, such as red Gingko, orchid Iris, and navy Hokusai Wave (see Figure 10-1). Visit www.oberondesign.com to find out more.

- **Drop-in/snap-in:** Drop the Kindle Paperwhite into a snap-in frame. The Amazon cover uses this design. Pad & Quill (www.padandquill.com) makes a wood and leather snap-in case that looks like a book when closed, as shown in Figure 10-2.

Figure 10-1: A variety of Kindles in Oberon cases.

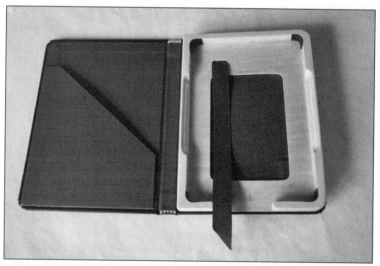

Figure 10-2: An empty Pad & Quill cover.

The Amazon cover

The cover from Amazon deserves special mention due to its unique feature: Open the cover and the Kindle Paperwhite turns on; close the cover and it puts the device to sleep. This "magic" is accomplished by a small magnet built into the corner of the case.

The cover is made of leather with a felt lining on the inside front cover and is available in seven colors. Figure 10-3 shows a Kindle Paperwhite inserted in the snap-in case — and sporting a vinyl skin from DecalGirl. (See the previous "Vinyl skins" section for details about this accessory.)

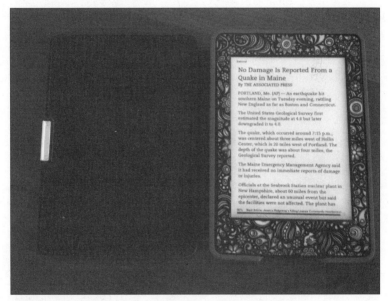

Figure 10-3: A Kindle Paperwhite secured in the Amazon cover.

Amazon recently introduced a cover that you can customize by adding a favorite photo. As of this writing, reviews on the appearance and attractiveness of the cover are mixed. Choosing a high-resolution photograph and realizing that the texture of the cover will show through seem to be key for customer satisfaction. You can learn more at this link: www.amazon.com/Kindle-Paperwhite-Black-Leather-Create/dp/B00DUQURNG/.

Protect your device from the elements

The Kindle Paperwhite is a delicate electronic device that can be damaged by moisture, dust, sand, or soot. If you regularly read at the beach or next to the pool, consider a plastic jacket or case to protect your device.

If you want to buy a protective cover, consider the Medium Whanganui case from Aquapac (`http://usstore.aquapac.net`). This case floats and is submersible up to 15 feet. The company offers free shipping on orders over $20. For an inexpensive alternative, put your Kindle Paperwhite in a plastic one-quart reclosable storage bag. You can still read the screen and navigate with the touchscreen.

If you put a small magnet in the corner of any cover with a front pocket (such as the one from Oberon), the cover will wake up your Kindle Paperwhite automatically when you open it and put it in Sleep mode when closed.

Sleeves and envelopes for naked reading

Do you prefer to read your Kindle Paperwhite without the encumbrance of a cover? If so, consider a sleeve or an envelope rather than a cover for protection.

If you're crafty, consider making your own sleeve! You can buy a pattern to make a Kindle sleeve from Birdiful Stitches. You can find details at `www.etsy.com/listing/55622726/padded-e-reader-sleeve-sewing-pattern`.

Sleeves are usually tight-fitting and may not have a zipper, snap, or other sort of closure device. They protect the Kindle when you aren't reading it — period. They don't have a place to attach a reading light or store the charger. On the plus side, sleeves are small and don't add a lot of bulk to your device. A Kindle Paperwhite in a sleeve can easily slip into a purse, messenger bag, or briefcase.

A variation on a sleeve is the less form-fitting envelope. As shown in Figure 10-4, BoxWave (`www.boxwave.com`) has taken the word *envelope* literally with its manila leather envelope, which looks like an envelope you'd receive in interoffice mail, right down to the red string closure.

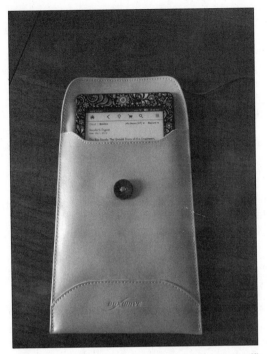

Figure 10-4: BoxWave's product looks like an interoffice envelope!

Zip into a jacket!

Many Kindle Paperwhite users choose a jacket for protection and convenience. *Jackets* are typically made of fabric, such as canvas or microfiber, and secure the device inside, usually by corner tabs. In addition, jackets have a zipper closure, which provides more security than a cover. Some jackets have extra features, such as a front pocket or a place to store the USB cable.

Jackets provide all-in-one security in a convenient, lightweight package. You can find a wide variety of jackets in the Kindle Store on Amazon. While on your computer, from the Search drop-down list, choose Kindle Store, type **accessories jackets** on the search bar, and click Go.

For $50, you can design your own jacket at M-Edge using your own artwork or photographs (www.medgestore.com).

Adding a Final Protective Layer

Many people don't consider their accessorizing complete until they add a bag or case to their Kindle Paperwhite's wardrobe. Bags range in size from petite — essentially a sleeve — to larger models that allow you to easily tote your Kindle, cover, charging cable, portable light, and whatever else you might have on hand. Unlike sleeves and jackets, bags and cases usually have a strap, such as a wristlet or a shoulder strap. You can also find fanny packs for your Kindle Paperwhite. Bags and cases are usually padded, adding one more layer of protection for the Kindle Paperwhite screen.

The popular Borsa Bella bags (www.borsabella.com) come in a variety of fabrics and sizes. The owner, Melissa Wisen, can even monogram your bag!

Adding the Finishing Touch

So far, I've described accessories that you put your Kindle Paperwhite in or accessories that go on your Kindle Paperwhite. In this section, I talk about external accessories: reading lights, styli, chargers, and more. Once again, you have plenty of options to choose from!

Portable reading lights

Unlike previous models of Kindles, the e-ink screen on the Kindle Paperwhite has a built-in integrated light, so an external light source is not required for reading. However, a portable reading light continues to be a popular accessory even for the Paperwhite. The variety of portable reading lights has boomed in recent years. If you opt to buy a light, the following suggestions will help you select the best one for your reading needs.

A reading light needs a power source. Rechargeable lights tend to be lighter and more expensive than lights that use batteries.

You can use rechargeable batteries in a battery-operated light, but you still have to contend with the added weight.

When checking out battery-operated lights, determine what type of battery is required. AA or AAA batteries cost less but weigh more than more specialized disk batteries.

No matter what sort of battery your light uses, always keep a spare set on hand.

A stylus for the touchscreen

Another accessory option for Kindle Paperwhite owners is a stylus for the touchscreen. Figure 10-5 shows a stylus alongside two other useful accessories, an adapter plug and a USB cable (described in the next section).

Figure 10-5: A stylus, an adapter plug, and a USB cable.

Why use a stylus? Some people prefer the more precise tip to tap the screen and menu options. A stylus can also keep the screen cleaner — no need to worry about dirt and oils on your fingers getting on the screen. If you're searching for a stylus, look for one that is designed to be used with a capacitive screen.

BoxWave (www.boxwave.com) makes a small bullet-style stylus with an attachment to hang on a keychain as well as a combo stylus with a ballpoint pen on one end and capacitive foam at the other. Amazon also sells a number of styli at a variety of price points. Just search for *Kindle stylus* in the Kindle Store.

Styli that work on the Kindle Fire (or other tablets) will work just fine on the Kindle Paperwhite.

Unlike the Kindle Touch, which used an infrared screen, the Kindle Paperwhite uses a capacitive screen. With an infrared screen, paired light beams and receptors sense when a finger, a stylus, or another object touches the screen and interrupts the light beam. The touch triggers an action, such as turning the page. Capacitive screens work with only a bare finger or a capacitive stylus. A capacitive screen uses a conductive layer on the underside of the screen through which a small amount of electricity flows. A touch on the screen causes a change in capacitance, which causes the desired action — usually turning the page on the Kindle Paperwhite. (In addition, the Kindle Paperwhite has a multitouch capacitive screen, which is why you can use two fingers to enlarge the font.) Although a stylus will work on a capacitive screen, a gloved finger will not.

Chargers and cables

Although the Kindle Paperwhite is advertised as having a very long battery life — up to two months if you only read 30 minutes per day with minimal wireless use and the light set at 10 — it still needs to be charged periodically.

The device ships with a USB cable that can be used for charging via a laptop or a computer. Simply connect the USB cable to the Paperwhite with the micro-USB adapter and then connect the other end of the cable to the computer. If you want to read the device while it is charging, eject it from the computer (but leave it physically attached). Instructions for how to do this are presented in Chapter 2.

The device doesn't ship with a plug adapter, but you can purchase one from Amazon for $9.99 (5 watts) or $19.99 (9 watts) or use one from an earlier model Kindle (Kindle 2 or Kindle Keyboard). You can also use a micro-USB plug adapter from another device, such as a BlackBerry.

The 9-watt charger is designed for the Kindle Fire but is approved for use in the Kindle Paperwhite. If you use this charger, the Kindle Paperwhite will charge completely in four hours or less.

Although the cable alone is sufficient, having a backup is a good idea, especially if you're prone to misplacing things. The complete unit — cable and plug — costs $25. The cable alone is $10.

Amazon sells plug adapters that work in the United Kingdom (Type G, UK), the European Union (EU Universal), and Australia (Type I, AU). If you regularly travel to any of these countries, buying an adapter specific for that region might be a worthwhile investment.

If you spend a lot of time in your car, consider a charger that plugs into the vehicle's power source/cigarette lighter. A variety of adapters that work with the Kindle Paperwhite are sold on Amazon.

Stands

Although the Kindle Paperwhite is light and easy to hold, sometimes you want to have your hands free while reading. In that case, you might find a stand to be a useful accessory. Amazon makes a basic minitravel stand that folds up and snaps shut when not in use. It's made of black plastic with rubber coated ends for stability. Learn more at `www.amazon.com/gp/product/B0064EL2DK/`.

BoxWave (`www.boxwave.com`) has two versions of easel-type bamboo devices: the stand and the panel. The stand is small, lightweight, and portable, whereas the panel separates into two pieces for storage. Note that BoxWave ships worldwide.

The Peeramid Pillow was designed by two sisters who wanted to bring comfortable reading to the world. Place the pyramid-shaped pillow on your lap, and fit the Kindle Paperwhite in the lip at the bottom of the pillow. When not in use, the pillow can be disguised as a traditional throw cushion on a couch or chair. Peeramid Pillows are sold in a variety of colors and fabric designs at Amazon (search for *Peeramid Pillow*).

Insuring Your Kindle Paperwhite

The Kindle Paperwhite comes with a one-year manufacturer's warranty that covers defects in materials and workmanship. Amazon also sells an extended warranty that covers the device for two full years, including damage caused from dropping it. The warranty, which is administered by SquareTrade, stays with the device even if you sell it or give it to someone, must be purchased within 30 days of purchasing your Kindle Paperwhite, and is available only to customers in the United States.

For details on the two-year warranty plan, tap the link on the right side of the main product page for the Kindle Paperwhite.

If your Kindle Paperwhite breaks and needs to be exchanged, return only the Kindle Paperwhite — don't send the USB cable. You'll receive another cable with your replacement.

Chapter 11

Troubleshooting

In This Chapter

▶ Finding help online

▶ Getting help from Amazon

▶ Troubleshooting common problems

▶ Resetting your Kindle Paperwhite

*M*ost people find that their Kindle Paperwhite is a reliable, problem-free device. For the infrequent occasions when glitches occur, they're usually resolved easily. In this chapter, I show you some troubleshooting tips that solve the most common difficulties encountered by Kindle Paperwhite owners.

For other, more complex, problems, I provide some steps you can take to solve them. First, though, I point you to ways you can get help from online resources, from other Kindle Paperwhite owners, and from Amazon's Kindle customer service.

Getting Help Online

Many Kindle owners join user forums, where a wide variety of problems can be addressed by helpful forum members. Amazon has a Kindle product forum that covers Kindle Paperwhite and all its e-reader devices. You can access the forum in several ways. The easiest is to go to the main Kindle Store on Amazon and choose Discussions, at the top of the page, as shown in Figure 11-1.

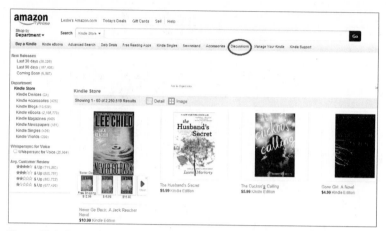

Figure 11-1: Accessing the Kindle Discussion forum at Amazon.

To find independent Kindle user forums, use your favorite search engine to search for *Kindle user forum.* Posting your Kindle Paperwhite problem in the troubleshooting area of an active forum can be an efficient way of resolving perplexing issues. Most forums have resident experts who have seen it all and can provide quick answers to common questions.

Amazon also provides a Kindle Support page with links to troubleshooting tips. Go to the Manage Your Kindle page at www.amazon.com/myk. (Note that you'll be prompted to log in to Amazon if you aren't already signed in.) From the Manage Your Kindle page, you can access Kindle Support through the Kindle Help link or the Kindle Support option, as shown in Figure 11-2.

Figure 11-2: You can access both Kindle Help and Kindle Support from this page.

The Kindle Support page includes a selection of how-to videos. From your computer, click the link for Helpful Kindle Support Videos and then click the Kindle Paperwhite (second generation) image to see the videos available for your device. These short videos cover 24 topics, including charging; toolbars and navigation; troubleshooting Wi-Fi; and syncing. The longest video is just over two minutes.

Your Kindle Paperwhite comes with the user guide already downloaded on the device. You can also download it from the Kindle Support page. To download a user guide in German, French, Italian, Spanish, Japanese, or Portuguese, go to your library through the Manage Your Kindle link (www.amazon.com/myk).

Contacting Amazon Kindle Customer Service

Kindle forums are full of appreciative reports about positive experiences with Amazon's Kindle customer service. These customer service representatives have a reputation for quickly resolving issues and for treating Kindle owners fairly and respectfully.

If your Kindle Paperwhite problem isn't readily resolved by basic troubleshooting steps, your best bet may be contacting customer service. More than likely, a ready resolution to your issue is waiting on the other end of the telephone line. The direct toll-free number for Kindle customer service is 1-866-321-8851. Customers outside the United States should call 1-206-266-0927.

From the Kindle Support page, you can choose to have a customer service representative call you. In this way, the representative can access your account before making the call, which might speed up the support process. You can also e-mail customer service or initiate a chat session from the Kindle Support page. Click the Contact Us button on the Kindle Support page to initiate help from Amazon by telephone, e-mail, or chat.

Common Problems and Solutions

In the following sections, I provide some of the more common problems reported by Kindle Paperwhite owners in community forums. For many of these problems, I provide steps for a quick resolution.

You see ghost images on the screen

Ghosting is the faint display of text or graphics that remains from a previous page even after you page forward.

This phenomenon may seem similar to the burn-in that can occur on older computer monitors — in which images of screensavers, for example, are permanently branded on the display. Fortunately, the e-ink screen doesn't burn in, and you can safely have your Kindle Paperwhite display a page or a screensaver for long periods of time.

If you encounter ghosting of a prior display on your Kindle Paperwhite, refresh the screen. To refresh the screen while reading an e-book or other content, tap near the top of the screen to display the toolbar, and then tap anywhere on the page. The display briefly flashes black as the screen refreshes and the toolbar disappears. From the Home screen, opening a book or other content causes the page to refresh — you'll know this is happening because the display briefly flashes black.

By default, your Kindle Paperwhite does a page refresh of its e-ink display every six pages. If you're experiencing ghosting issues, change the setting to have the display refresh with every page turn. Tap Menu⇨Settings⇨Reading Options. Set the Page Refresh option to On.

Having the page refresh on every page turn uses more battery power.

The device freezes or is very slow

If your Kindle Paperwhite stops behaving in its usual speedy fashion or freezes, you can typically resolve the problem by doing a menu restart or a hard restart.

Begin by performing a menu restart on your Kindle Paperwhite:

1. **Tap Menu⇨Settings.**

2. **Tap Menu⇨Restart.**

   (Restart is the third item on the drop-down menu that appears.) Your Kindle Paperwhite displays the start-up screen and a progress bar. After a minute or so, the device restarts and displays the Home screen.

If the menu restart doesn't resolve the problem, try a hard restart:

1. **Press and hold down the power button for 7 to 15 seconds.**

   A pop-up menu appears, as shown in Figure 11-3.

2. **Tap Restart.**

   The start-up screen appears with a silhouetted child reading under a tree. In a few seconds, the device begins the restart process and displays a progress bar. When that restart is complete, you see the Home screen.

Power		
Please select from the following options:		
Cancel	Restart	Screen Off

Figure 11-3: The hard restart menu.

 Sometimes a low battery can be the cause of unexpected Kindle Paperwhite behavior. If you continue to have problems, plug in your device to let it charge for at least an hour and then try a menu restart again, followed by a hard restart if necessary.

The device is behaving erratically

If your Kindle Paperwhite is exhibiting erratic behavior, such as difficulty downloading content or jumping from section to section in a book instead of moving smoothly from page to page, try a hard restart. Simply follow the directions in the preceding section. A hard restart is easy and resolves many glitches.

You can't connect to Wi-Fi automatically

The Kindle Paperwhite automatically scans for Wi-Fi networks that are in range of your device. If one (or more) networks are found, the device will connect automatically. If a password is required, a screen appears asking you to input that information. Generally, the process is quick and easy.

Occasionally, however, you may need to connect to the Wi-Fi network manually. Follow these steps:

1. **Tap Menu⇨Settings.**

2. **If the network to which you want to connect appears in the list, tap that network.**

   You're finished!

3. **If the network to which you want to connect doesn't appear in the list:**

   a. **Tap Other (at the bottom of the Wi-Fi Networks box).**

      A dialog box named Enter Wi-Fi Network appears, along with the on-screen keyboard.

   b. **Using the onscreen keyboard, enter the network name and, if applicable, the password.**

   c. **Tap the Advanced button.**

   d. **Work through the series of screens, entering information related to the network, including connection type, IP address, and security type.**

      Advance through the screens by using the up and down arrows.

      If necessary, contact the person who set up the network for assistance with filling in this information.

   e. **When all the necessary information has been entered, tap the Connect button to join the network.**

If your Kindle Paperwhite is connected to your home network but can't connect to Amazon, you may need to reestablish the connection. Tap Menu⇨Settings⇨Wi-Fi Networks, and then tap the network that has a check mark to its left. When the Forget Network? dialog box appears, tap Forget. You'll have to reselect the network and enter the password (if one is required).

If you're having trouble connecting to your home network, unplug the Wi-Fi router, wait at least 60 seconds, and then plug it in and wait for the network to restart.

The battery discharges quickly

Amazon advertises that a single charge of the battery in the Kindle Paperwhite should last eight weeks, based on a half-hour of reading each day with minimal use of the wireless and the light set at 10. For voracious readers (like me), that usage is slight. Still, the battery should last at least a week or two even with daily usage with the wireless turned on.

If you notice that the battery is running down in a short period of time (48 to 72 hours), the problem may be due to unindexed content. Typically, whenever you add content to the Kindle Paperwhite, it indexes the material. This allows you to search for words or terms both within a specific book as well as across all content on the device.

Occasionally, a book fails to index properly, so the device tries endlessly (and unsuccessfully) to index it, causing the battery to run down. To determine whether this is the problem, take the following steps:

1. **From the Home screen, tap the Search icon.**

2. **Make sure that All Text is displayed to the right of the search box.**

   If it isn't, tap the phrase that does appear to open a drop-down menu and select All Text — the second choice in the list.

3. **Type an unusual word or just a string of letters.**

   Don't choose a common word such as *man* or *the*.

4. **Tap the arrow next to the box to begin the search.**

5. **Check for unindexed items.**

   Look below the list of search results (if any) for Items Not Yet Indexed. (To see what a successful search screen looks like, see Chapter 4.) Tap the Items Not Yet Indexed line to see the items that haven't been indexed.

6. **If you have an unindexed item, remove it by pressing and holding down on it and then selecting Delete from the menu that appears.**

   If you've acquired this content from Amazon, it will be available to you for redownloading from the Cloud. For other content, make sure you have a backup. Samples from Amazon must be redownloaded from the book's Amazon page, so make a note of those before deleting, if you want to resample that content.

7. **Charge your battery completely.**

Make a note of the date and keep track of how long it takes the battery to discharge. You may have to wait a few days to see whether the battery problem has resolved. When you've determined that the battery is functioning normally, you can put the offending (unindexed) items back on your Kindle Paperwhite by redownloading from the Cloud, sideloading from your computer, or resampling the content from Amazon.

If more than one item appeared on the unindexed content list and you want to put these items back on your Kindle Paperwhite, add them one at a time and wait for each to finish indexing before adding the next. In this way, if a problem exists with specific content, you can more easily identify which book is the offender.

If you continue to have problems, contact customer service using the steps described in the previous section, "Contacting Amazon Kindle Customer Service."

Your Paperwhite doesn't sync among devices

Normally, you can start reading an e-book on one device, such as your Kindle Paperwhite, and continue reading from where you left off on another device.

Amazon's Whispersync feature enables you to move seamlessly from reading on your Kindle Paperwhite to reading on a smartphone or your computer, as shown in Figure 11-4. In addition, Whispersync for Voice allows you to sync between your Kindle Paperwhite and an Audible version of a book that you listen to on your preferred audio device with the Audible app.

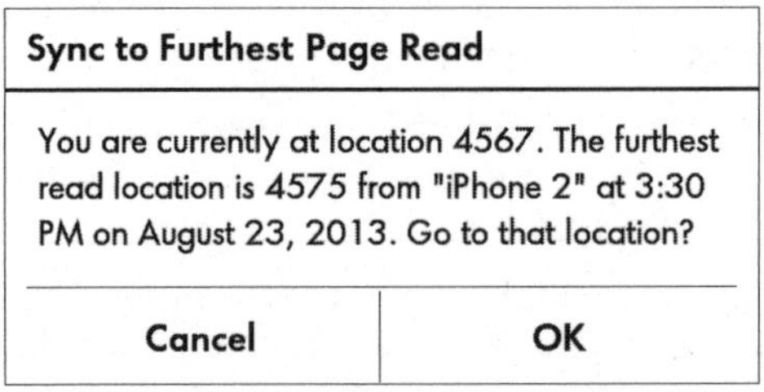

Sync to Furthest Page Read
You are currently at location 4567. The furthest read location is 4575 from "iPhone 2" at 3:30 PM on August 23, 2013. Go to that location?

Cancel	OK

Figure 11-4: The Sync screen between a Paperwhite and an iPhone.

When opening the e-book on the other device, you're typically prompted with the option to move to the furthest location read (refer to Figure 11-4). If this doesn't happen, check the following:

- ✔ **Connection to Amazon's servers:** For Whispersync to work, the devices must be connected to Amazon's servers. Ensure that your Kindle Paperwhite or other device has Wi-Fi or 3G connectivity when syncing.

- ✔ **Synchronization setting:** If your devices are connected to Amazon's servers and synchronization still isn't working, check your synchronization settings. Log in to Amazon and go to the Manage Your Kindle page (www.amazon.com/myk).

Look at the left column and scroll down to the Whispersync Device Synchronization link. Choose that link, and verify that the Synchronization option is set to On.

The Synchronization setting affects *all* devices and all content associated with your account; you can't selectively turn Device Synchronization on or off for a particular device or for a particular e-book. If you have multiple Kindles on your account (for example, Kindles that belong to you, your spouse, and your children) and everyone is reading the same e-book, the Kindle synchronizes to the last page read for everyone. In this case, you may want to turn off synchronization.

You can reset the last page read from Your Kindle Library at Manage Your Kindle. Next to the appropriate title, click the Actions box. From the drop-down menu that appears, select Clear Furthest Page Read.

If your device is still having synchronization problems, try exiting the book to the Home screen — rather than leaving the book open when the Kindle Paperwhite goes into Sleep mode.

An e-book won't open or stops responding

If your Kindle Paperwhite freezes or starts behaving strangely when you're reading a particular e-book or other content, try a menu restart and then, if necessary, a hard restart. For directions, see "The device freezes or is very slow" section, earlier in this chapter.

If those solutions don't work, the file might be corrupted and removing the item might solve the problem. However, if the book came from a source other than Amazon, you should have a backup before deleting it from your Kindle Paperwhite. If you bought the book from Amazon, it will be stored in the Cloud and you can redownload it to your device.

Remove the item and then restart your Kindle Paperwhite by following these steps:

1. **From the Home screen, tap and hold down on the item.**

   A pop-up menu appears, with several options.

2. **Tap the Remove from Device option or, for samples, the Delete This Sample option.**

   The e-book or sample is removed from your Kindle Paperwhite.

3. **Restart your Kindle Paperwhite by pressing and holding the power button for 7–15 seconds and tapping Restart on the pop-up menu that appears.**

Try reading other content to see whether the symptoms have cleared up. If so, you can try downloading the e-book again from Amazon by selecting it from the Cloud on your Home screen or sideloading it to your device from your computer. If none of these steps work, contact customer service using the steps described in the previous section, "Contacting Amazon Kindle Customer Service."

A downloaded item doesn't appear on the Home screen

At times, an item you've downloaded wirelessly or transferred by USB to your Kindle Paperwhite doesn't appear on your Home screen. Usually the Kindle Paperwhite refreshes its content listing immediately when new content is added. But if that doesn't happen, tap Menu from the Home screen and then tap Sync and Check for Items. If that doesn't work, try a menu restart, as described in "The device freezes or is very slow" section, earlier in this chapter. This action forces your Kindle to refresh its content listing.

 If you've transferred content to your Kindle via USB, make sure the content is in the Documents folder on your device. If you've inadvertently placed an e-book in the root directory, it won't appear on your Home screen.

The Home screen displays items out of order

You can display items on your Home screen by Recent, Title, Author, or Collections. Occasionally, items aren't displayed in the correct order.

To resolve this problem, do a quick resync:

1. **From the Home screen, tap the Menu icon.**
2. **Tap Sync and Check for Items.**

   Sync and Check for Items is the fourth option on the drop-down menu. Your Home screen displays items in proper order.

Make sure the clock on your Kindle Paperwhite is set to the correct time. If the clock is not accurate, the device will not sync properly, resulting in a Home page with books not listed in the proper order. To set the time, tap Menu⇨Settings⇨Device Options⇨Device Time.

You can set the Kindle Paperwhite 3G to update the clock automatically. On a Wi-Fi–only Kindle Paperwhite, you must set the clock manually. Keep this fact in mind when traveling or if you live in an area with daylight saving time.

The device doesn't recognize your password

You can use a password to protect access to your Kindle Paperwhite. If the password that you set for your device isn't working, you have some troubleshooting options:

- ✔ **Be sure you enter the password correctly.**

- ✔ **Try some variations of the password.** Maybe you mistyped it (twice) when you originally set it up.

- ✔ **If you have more than one Kindle in your household, make sure you enter the password on the right device.** Sorry, I have to include this one!

I hope one of these troubleshooting steps helps because the next remedy — resetting your password — is drastic. This solution wipes all content from your Kindle Paperwhite and deregisters it from Amazon. Reinstalling all your books, personal documents, and collection can be done, but it takes time.

To reset your password, type **111222777** in the Password field and then tap OK. Your Kindle is wiped clean. You now have to register the device again with Amazon (as detailed in Chapter 2) and download content again as desired from your Amazon archive, either by using the Cloud or pushing content to your Kindle Paperwhite (see Chapter 5).

An e-book you purchased hasn't downloaded from the Kindle Store

You've purchased an e-book — or some other content — from the Kindle Store, and it hasn't appeared on your Home screen. Or perhaps your subscription content doesn't load automatically.

If you don't see content that should be downloaded, try these tips:

- **If you have a Wi-Fi–only Kindle Paperwhite, make sure it's connected to a Wi-Fi network.** If it is, you'll see the Wi-Fi indicator in the top-right corner of the Home screen. The device must be connected to Wi-Fi to download e-books and other content from the Kindle Store.

- **If you have a Kindle Paperwhite 3G, ensure that it's either connected to a Wi-Fi network or in a 3G coverage area.** The bars at the top of the Home screen indicate the strength of the 3G signal. If the 3G signal is weak (two bars or less), Kindle Store connectivity may be slow or disrupted.

  If your Kindle Paperwhite is adequately connected via Wi-Fi or 3G but you're still having trouble downloading content, try this: From the Home screen, tap the Menu icon and select Sync and Check for Items.

- **Ensure that the battery is charged sufficiently.** When the battery level is low, connectivity may be affected. If the battery charge meter, which is displayed in the top-right corner of the Home screen, is less than 25 percent, plug in your Kindle Paperwhite and let it charge for a few hours.

- **Make sure the e-book is in your library at Amazon.** When you make a purchase, you receive a confirmation e-mail from Amazon. If you don't receive the e-mail and the book doesn't appear in your library, you may not have successfully completed the purchase. In that case, buy the book again. If the problem persists, contact customer service (see "Contacting Amazon Kindle Customer Service," earlier in the chapter).

If you can't find a book, make sure it isn't somewhere unexpected on your Kindle. Change the sort order to By Author or Recent. If you are redownloading a book that was previously placed in a collection on your Kindle Paperwhite, it will redownload to that collection.

Another reason why an e-book might not download to your Kindle is a problem or delay with Amazon's servers. Try waiting for a few hours and see whether the e-book downloads eventually.

What to Do as a Last Resort

If all else fails, you can reset your Kindle Paperwhite back to factory specifications.

A factory reset is also a way to wipe your Kindle Paperwhite clean if you ever decide to give it as a gift or sell it.

Resetting your Kindle Paperwhite is a last-resort step. Before you carry out a factory reset, try the more common and less drastic fixes described in the "Common Problems and Solutions" section, earlier in this chapter. Also, consider calling Amazon Kindle customer service before undertaking a factory reset on your own. (See "Contacting Amazon Kindle Customer Service," earlier in the chapter.)

To reset your Kindle Paperwhite to its original out-of-the-box state, follow these steps:

1. **Tap Menu⇨Settings.**

2. **Tap Menu⇨>Reset Device.**

3. **When you see the warning, tap Yes. (To back out without resetting, you'd tap No.)**

   Your Kindle Paperwhite resets. You have to re-register the device with Amazon and download your Kindle e-books and other content from the Cloud at your Amazon account. You also need to retransfer any personal documents that you've loaded on your Kindle Paperwhite from your computer.

Personal documents that you have sent to your Kindle Paperwhite via e-mail are stored in the Cloud at your Amazon account. You can transfer these documents to your Kindle Paperwhite just like any other content stored in the Cloud.

If you have a Wi-Fi–only Kindle Paperwhite, be sure to have the Wi-Fi password for your router. You'll need that password to connect the device to the wireless service. Without a Wi-Fi or 3G connection, you won't be able to transfer content.

Chapter 12

Ten Helpful Kindle Paperwhite Tips

. . . .

In This Chapter

▶ Be a bargain hunter

▶ Personalize your device

▶ Be clever with collections

▶ Have fun with words

▶ Keep your device safe

▶ Fly with your Kindle Paperwhite

▶ Drive with your Kindle Paperwhite

▶ Troubleshoot your device

▶ Give great gifts

▶ Convert a friend

. . . .

In trademark *For Dummies* style, this chapter contains ten tips to make your Kindle Paperwhite more useful. These concise and easy-to-digest tips can benefit power users and casual readers alike.

Be a Bargain Hunter

Many people ask if you can buy an e-book version of a previously purchased printed book for free or for a reduced price. Until November 2013, the answer to that question was no — but then Amazon introduced Kindle Matchbook. This program allows you to buy e-books of print books you've previously purchased on Amazon. (Not all books are in the program.) If you've been a loyal Amazon customer, you probably have many books on your shelf that will qualify for this program.

You can search for other bargains in addition to Matchbook. Amazon has a Daily Deal, where you can buy current popular books at deeply discounted prices, often $1.99 or less. These deals last only a day, so make sure to take advantage of them when you see ones you want.

To find out about free books, peruse the Top 100 Free Books at the main page of the Kindle Store. This list is updated hourly and new free books appear on a regular basis, so be sure to check the list often.

Kindle First is another program that allows you to get one new release per month for $1.99 or free for Amazon Prime customers. You may choose from four books selected from Amazon Editions. To find out more, go to www.amazon.com/gp/digital/kindle/ botm/?tag=viglink126429-20. Sign up for the monthly newsletter to be alerted to the choices on the first of the month.

Whispersync for Voice allows you to read a Kindle Paperwhite book and listen to an Audible book at the same time. When you switch between devices, you can pick up where you left off in the other version. Many Audible books are offered at discounted prices if you own the Kindle version, often $3.95 or less (the usual price is generally over $20). If the Audible version is available at a reduced price, it will say so on the Kindle version's product page.

Personalize Your Device

Make your Kindle Paperwhite unique. Here are two tips to personalize your Kindle Paperwhite so that everyone knows it's yours:

- ✔ **Name your device.** Give your Kindle Paperwhite a special name that reflects your — and its — personality. Perhaps you want to give your Kindle Paperwhite a character's name from a favorite book, a name you love (or even wish you had), or a meaningful phrase. I know of a Kindle Paperwhite named *Catalyst* because it's a catalyst for reading. To change the device name, tap Menu⇨Settings to display Device Options, and make your change. You can name your device also on Amazon's Manage Your Kindle area (www.amazon.com/myk).

- ✔ **Change the font and font size.** The Kindle Paperwhite has six fonts. Play around with them to find the one that's most comfortable for your eyes. *Note:* You have to be in an e-book (or other content) to choose the font options. While reading a book, tap the top region of the screen to display the toolbar. Tap the Text (Aa) icon, on the left of the toolbar, and then tap through the eight font sizes, six fonts (Baskerville, Caecilia, Caecilia Condensed, Futura, Helvetica, and Palatino), line spacing, and margins. (See Chapter 2 for details.)

Be Clever with Collections

Many readers organize their Kindle Paperwhite e-books into collections so that they can quickly find their favorites among the dozens — or even hundreds — of books stored on the device. Although names such as Bestsellers and Finished are serviceable, why not have some fun? Here are a few suggestions culled from Kindle users:

- Once Upon a Time (young adult/children)
- Books that Make Me Look Smart (classics)
- Small Servings (samples)
- On the Nightstand (currently reading)
- On the Docket (coming up next)
- What Was I Thinking? DNF (did not finish)
- Maybe Someday (all unread books)
- Can't Resist a Bargain (cheap or freebies)
- Tell Me about Your Life (autobiographies and biographies)
- A Blast from the Past (historical fiction)
- Magic and Mayhem (fantasy and paranormal)
- Future Bestsellers (books from indie authors)
- Extra! Extra! (subscription content, such as newspapers and magazines)
- Let's Eat! (cookbooks)
- Technical Manuals (guilty pleasures and erotica)

Have Fun with Words

Here are a few tips for having fun with words on your Kindle Paperwhite:

- **Use the dictionary to look up unfamiliar words.** Simply press and hold down on a word. The dictionary definition appears automatically.

- **Share new words on Facebook or Twitter.** From the dictionary definition, tap More, tap Share, add a note, and tap Share. The information will be posted to your Facebook page and Twitter feed. A notation (superscripted number) will also be linked to the passage on your Kindle Paperwhite.

✓ **Translate words into another language.** The Kindle Paperwhite allows you to translate words (and phrases) into sixteen languages, including Chinese (simplified and traditional), Hindi, and Russian. Press and hold down on the word. From the dictionary definition page, tap More, and then tap Translation. On the screen that appears, tap To: English to see the list of languages and choose one. (To see the entire list, drag it up and down with your finger.)

✓ **Translate words into English.** Are you reading a book that contains words or phrases in another language? You can translate them to English. The Kindle Paperwhite will even detect the source language!

✓ **Use Vocabulary Builder to learn new words.** Every word you look up in the dictionary is added to a list in Vocabulary Builder. Tap Vocabulary Builder from the Home screen to access the list. For each word, its dictionary definition and usage will be displayed. After you've committed a word to memory, tap Mastered to remove it from the list.

✓ **Play Every Word.** Every Word is a fun word-building game designed for the Kindle and available for free from Amazon.

Keep Your Device Safe

The following list provides tips for keeping your Kindle Paperwhite safe and in working order:

✓ **Don't drop the device.** A drop from just a few feet can be enough to destroy the screen. Treat the device carefully and try to prevent drops.

✓ **Keep the device away from water.** The Kindle Paperwhite and water don't mix. A spill into the tub or pool is a sure way to turn your Kindle Paperwhite into a paperweight. If you want to use your Kindle Paperwhite in watery environments, protect it. Many users report that heavy duty Ziploc bags work well. Others opt for custom waterproof jackets, such as those sold by M-Edge. (See Chapter 10 for details.) Even with protection, however, the device can be damaged if an accident occurs.

✓ **Keep the device clean.** Sand or dust can damage the internal circuitry and make your Kindle Paperwhite unusable. If you opt to read at the beach or the Mojave, protect your Kindle Paperwhite with a bag or a plastic jacket. A can of compressed air is great for getting dust out of the corners of your Kindle Paperwhite, too.

✔ **Don't use, store, or charge the device in extreme temperatures.** By *extreme,* I mean below 32°F or above 95°F (0°C to 35°C). Outside these temperatures, the e-ink display might become damaged. If you're waiting on an elevated platform on a frigidly cold day in Chicago, keep your Kindle Paperwhite in your briefcase, warm and protected.

✔ **Keep the device in a cover, sleeve, or jacket.** Even if you prefer to hold the Kindle Paperwhite without a cover for reading, keep it covered when you're not using it to protect the screen. You can find many attractive covers, sleeves, and jackets from simple to fashion-forward, from inexpensive to pricey. To keep your Kindle Paperwhite safe, consider this important investment. See Chapter 10 for accessories.

✔ **Don't let young children handle the device.** Many people ask, "How old does a child need to be to use a Kindle Paperwhite?" If children are old enough to read books with chapters, they're probably old enough to handle a Kindle Paperwhite with minimal supervision. Children younger than 5 might not understand that the Kindle Paperwhite is delicate and needs to be treated gently. To be on the safe side, keep your Kindle Paperwhite out of their hands completely.

✔ **Protect your Kindle Paperwhite from your pets.** Keep your device safe from canine and feline friends. I've heard of dogs chewing a Kindle Paperwhite to pieces and cats walking across — and cracking — the screen.

✔ **Don't leave your Kindle Paperwhite on a chair or bed.** It's easy to sit on your Kindle Paperwhite, roll over on it, or put your elbow through the display.

Fly with Your Kindle Paperwhite

The Kindle Paperwhite is the perfect traveling companion, helping you get through hours of waiting in airports. And for those people who catch up on overdue reading during their vacation, the Kindle Paperwhite is ideal.

The following tips will help make your trips smooth and trouble-free:

✔ **Use common sense for airport security and screening.** Take the Kindle Paperwhite out of your bag or carry-on and put it in the screening bin, along with your cellphone and any other electronic devices. The Kindle Paperwhite needs to be turned off, the wireless needs to be turned off, and the device must be in Airplane mode (see Chapter 2). Many ask if x-ray screening can damage a Kindle; I've traveled with my Paperwhite throughout the United States and abroad without any problems.

✓ **Don't leave your Kindle Paperwhite in the seat pocket of the plane.** In every sad story I've heard of a Kindle left on a plane, it was left in the seat pocket. Don't tempt fate. Keep your Kindle Paperwhite in your purse, briefcase, backpack, or carry-on when you aren't reading it.

✓ **If you are requested to do so, turn off the Kindle Paperwhite during takeoff and landing.** In the eyes of the FAA, the Kindle Paperwhite is a portable electronic device and must be turned off (not just in Sleep mode) for takeoff and landing. To turn off the device, press down on the power button for 7–15 seconds and choose the Screen Off option in the menu that appears. Then, when the announcement is made that it's safe to use portable electronic devices, you can take out your Kindle Paperwhite, tap Menu⇨Settings, and then toggle Airplane mode to On.

Until November 2013, airline passengers were required to turn off their Kindles (all models, including the Kindle Paperwhite) during takeoff and landing and any time the plane was flying at less than 10,000 feet. However, the FAA has recently amended its rules to expand the use of personal electronic devices during all phases of a flight — they hope to provide passengers with a "gate-to-gate" reading, gaming, and video-watching experience. Each airline carrier will be able to decide individually how to implement these new rules. As a result, things will be "up in the air" for several months as airlines decide how to proceed. Listen carefully to all announcements from the flight attendants and pilot and, if required, turn off your Kindle during takeoff and landing.

✓ **Never turn on 3G on airplane.** Even though you can read a Kindle Paperwhite while flying, 3G (if your Kindle Paperwhite is so equipped) must be turned off, as with a cellphone. If the airline provides in-flight Wi-Fi, you can turn on the wireless on a Wi-Fi–only Kindle Paperwhite when the flight attendant or pilot allows it.

✓ **Make sure you have the proper charging equipment when traveling.** The Kindle Paperwhite ships with only a USB cord. You can use this to charge your device from your computer, but it's a good idea to have a plug adapter, too, so you don't rely on only one charging option. If you're traveling outside the United States, you'll need a plug adapter if you want to charge your Kindle Paperwhite from an electrical socket.

The Kindle Paperwhite is a dual-voltage device, so you do not need a converter.

If you regularly travel to the same country, consider buying a plug specific to that area. See Chapter 10 for details.

✔ **Load your Kindle Paperwhite with reading content before you leave.** The Kindle Paperwhite works internationally, so Wi-Fi and 3G should work everywhere. Even so, take some time before your trip to dig out e-books from the archive or buy some e-books from your wish list. Then while you're traveling, you'll have dozens of e-books available at your fingertips — without worrying about buying or downloading them.

If you're planning a cruise, realize that Wi-Fi access can be expensive, amounting to a surcharge on every Kindle Paperwhite e-book you download. Now you have an even more compelling reason to load up your device before you leave!

Drive with Your Kindle Paperwhite

If you travel a lot by car, consider getting a car charger. Then you won't need to charge your Kindle Paperwhite in a hotel room, which means you'll have less chance of leaving the power cord, plug, and even Kindle Paperwhite behind. You can find a variety of Kindle Paperwhite–compatible car chargers at different price points on Amazon.

If you frequently travel by car, consider getting a Kindle/Audible audiobook bundle to use with your preferred audio device. Whispersync for Voice makes it easy to listen to a book while you're driving. When the day's driving is done, you can pick up your Kindle Paperwhite and sync to the last place you listened to on the audio device.

Troubleshoot Your Device

Having trouble with your Kindle Paperwhite? Following are some of the most common resolutions to Kindle Paperwhite issues:

✔ **Turn your Kindle Paperwhite off and then on again.** Many Kindle Paperwhite issues will resolve themselves by simply cycling your Kindle Paperwhite off and then on. Turn off the device by holding down the power button for 7 to 15 seconds and choosing Screen Off from the menu that appears. Then turn on your Kindle Paperwhite by pressing and releasing the power button.

- **Restart your Kindle Paperwhite using the menu.** Try restarting your Kindle Paperwhite through the menu system. Tap Menu⇨Settings⇨Menu⇨Restart.

- **Perform a hard restart of your Kindle Paperwhite.** Hold down the power button for 7 to 15 seconds and then choose Restart from the menu that appears. You'll see the Kindle logo with a progress bar. When the restart is completed, your Home page is displayed on the screen.

- **Make sure your Kindle Paperwhite is fully charged.** Many users have reported a variety of issues ranging from books not downloading to problems with syncing when the battery charge drops below 25 percent. If you're having problems and the battery indicator is low, plug in your Kindle Paperwhite and let it recharge to full strength.

- **Contact customer service.** Amazon provides fantastic customer service for its entire family of Kindle devices. If the preceding tips haven't solved your problem, call customer service at their direct toll-free number: 1-866-321-8851 (in the United States). U.S. Amazon customers traveling outside the United States should call 1-206-266-0927. You can also e-mail customer service or chat online with a customer service representative. Go to the Kindle support page at `www.amazon.com/gp/help/contact-us/kindle-help.html`? for the necessary links, including information for non-U.S. customers.

Give Great Gifts

You love your Kindle Paperwhite and so does your best friend. So what do you get your friend for a gift? An Amazon gift card or e-book!

You can send an electronic Amazon gift card in any amount up to $2,000. You can select a design that's specific to the Kindle Paperwhite or a design that reflects the season or occasion. Log in to your Amazon account and click Purchase a Gift Card to get started. To give a Kindle Paperwhite e-book as a gift, search the Kindle Store for one; then select the Give as a Gift option on the purchase page and go from there. You need to know the recipient's e-mail address to complete either transaction.

Another great gift is a 3-, 6-, or 12-month membership at Audible.com. A membership allows your recipient to buy audiobooks and synchronize them between an audio device and the

Kindle Paperwhite for a combined reading and listening experience. To find out more, visit the Gift Center at www.audible.com.

Following are some other great gifts for fellow Kindle Paperwhite owners.

- A plug adapter (the device ships with only a USB cord)
- An extra USB cord
- A cover, sleeve, jacket, or skin
- A capacitive stylus to use on the touchscreen

For more information on all these, see Chapter 10.

Convert a Friend

Most people who experience a Kindle Paperwhite become quite enamored with it and, as a result, want to convert their friends and relatives. Consider the following when trying to help a non-Kindle Paperwhite user see the light:

- **The Kindle app can be used on a computer, an iPad, or a smartphone.** The Kindle application is free, and versions are available for a computer as well as BlackBerry, Android, iPad, and iPhone devices. Reading Kindle e-books on a device with the Kindle app is a good first step to understanding the Kindle Paperwhite experience. With the app, a user can buy e-books from Amazon and create an archive of titles. (Realize that with the app, you'll be reading on a device with an LCD screen. You need to have a Kindle Paperwhite or other Kindle e-reader if you want the e-ink experience.) If the user gets a Kindle Paperwhite, the e-books in the archive are available for downloading to the device. In addition, the app synchronizes among devices, so if you read a few pages on, say, your iPhone and then switch to the Kindle Paperwhite, it synchronizes to the last page read.

- **The Kindle Paperwhite is environmentally friendly.** Printed books require paper for printing, packaging for shipping, and trucks for hauling, which are all valuable resources that cost money and are potentially harmful to the environment. E-books, which consume a few electrons and are delivered via wireless, are an ecologically wise choice for reading.

- **The Kindle Paperwhite is hypoallergenic.** Some people are allergic to the ink used in printed books. Over time, printed books can become dirty or infested with dust mites, which are also potent allergens. E-books have no such irritants, so they're a good choice for readers with allergies.

- ✔ **A Kindle Paperwhite can help decrease clutter and save space.** Face it, books take up a lot of room in your home. You can store an entire library (1,100 e-books) in a device that you can hold in your hand. Plus, you can store thousands more books in the Cloud.

- ✔ **A Kindle Paperwhite library can never be destroyed in a fire or flood.** Although a Kindle Paperwhite might break or become damaged, your Kindle Paperwhite library, stored in the Cloud at your Amazon account, will always be available.

- ✔ **You can save money on e-book purchases.** A Kindle Paperwhite requires an initial investment, but e-books are generally less expensive than their printed counterparts. In addition, you can find many sources of free e-books as well as frequent free e-book promotions.

- ✔ **You can change the font size, making reading easier.** After you discover the convenience of enlarging or reducing the font to accommodate your eyes or the lighting conditions, you'll realize the inconvenience of reading very small print. Many people with vision problems have been able to regain their joy of reading by using the Kindle Paperwhite with enlarged fonts.

- ✔ **You can make annotations without harming the e-book.** The Kindle Paperwhite allows you to make notes, highlight passages, and annotate important sections, all without leaving permanent marks in the book. This is good for the e-book and good for other readers, who may be interested in the content but not in your notes.

- ✔ **Share your reading accomplishments.** Use social media, such as Goodreads, Facebook, and Twitter, to share your reviews and ratings of the books you read, right from the book.

- ✔ **Improve your vocabulary by using the dictionary to look up unfamiliar words.** When you were learning to read, you might have looked up words you didn't know in the dictionary. But as you got older, you might have left that habit behind. The Kindle Paperwhite makes looking up unfamiliar words easy. Instead of trying to puzzle out what *unctuous* means, look it up! (By the way, *unctuous* means smooth and greasy in texture or appearance.)

- ✔ **Keep your reading list private.** You might not want others to know that you're reading *The Bald Duke's Secret Mistress*. Everyone has guilty pleasures — is it really anyone else's business that you like to read bodice rippers or trashy celebrity biographies?

Index